SHADOW OF DEATH

by

Lilli Schultze

FOREWORD

by

Thomas R. Nickel

ROSEDALE CHRISTIAN BOOKS
11035 Chapman Road
Rosedale, BC V0X 1X2
(604) 794-7434

Christian Light Publications
Harrisonburg, Virginia 22802

SHADOW OF DEATH

Christian Light Publications, Inc., Harrisonburg, Virginia 22802

© 1981 by Christian Light Publications, Inc.
All rights reserved. Published 1981
Printed in the United States of America

4th printing, 2008

Cover Art: Martha Yoder

ISBN 978-0-87813-516-5

FOREWORD

I have written, edited and published countless human interest and miracle stories, but none more revealing of the Father's hand than this account of the life of Lilli Schultze.

As I followed Lilli's episodes from her teenage girlhood in Germany, through Hitler's Satan-inspired war of destruction and suffering, to her ultimate residence in America, I lived her experiences along with her, absorbed in the details of her description.

The American consul in Germany told Lilli when he arranged for her to leave for America: "When you have arrived in America, be sure to write a book about your life. The American people will be interested in reading it."

Lilli has written the book, and you are having the opportunity to read it. I am sure it will leave as deep an impression upon you as it did on me, and you, too, will see the Father's hand revealed throughout its pages.

—Thomas R. Nickel

DEDICATION

I would like to dedicate this book
To my Papa, who has been missing since
   World War II,
To my Uncle and Aunt, Mr. and Mrs. George
   Buchholz, who, as our sponsors, were
   instrumental in bringing Mother and
   her three children to America,
To the American people for the love and consideration shown to our family.
To my heavenly Father, Jesus my Saviour,
   and the precious Holy Spirit, whom I
   wish to honor above all others with this
   account.

> My mouth shall speak the
> praise of the Lord: and let
> all flesh bless his holy
> name for ever and ever.
> Psalm 145:21.

ACKNOWLEDGEMENTS

My words cannot express the joy and thankfulness that have been mine, for the help of my dear Aunt Lisa who has spent countless hours with me, helping me while I was writing. I am also very grateful to Ida B. Bontrager, author of several books, school teacher and minister's wife, for taking time to edit this book. Finally, I am so grateful for the prayers, encouragement, and love from all of my dear friends. May God bless everyone who has had a part in this effort.

—The Author

INTRODUCTION

I never buy a book until I have read the introduction. You might feel the same way, so let me share with you why I have written this account.

I am of German descent. I came to America in 1951 from the German province of Westfalen, near the River Rhine. I do count it a privilege to live in this great country of America, where I can enjoy real freedom.

While my family and I were still in Germany, we were invited by an American consul for an interview. He asked us many questions, among them why we wanted to immigrate to America. We told him our life story. He advised me, "When you have arrived in America, be sure to write a book. The American people will be much interested in reading it."

After we arrived, however, I had to learn the English language.

Soon I began receiving invitations to speak to various church women's groups. I found people greatly interested in my life story, and I was again advised to write a book. I promised the Lord that I would do anything that would honor and glorify His name. I decided that writing a book was the way for me to

6

convey to others the burden of my heart.

I am sure there is a reason why God spared my life and the lives of my family. We know it was only by a miracle that we were brought to the United States of America.

I began to pray about the book, asking myself the question, "Would I be able to express myself just as I feel in my heart?" I felt too weak and unlearned to write a book in the English language. Then the Lord gave me a scripture, "But God hath chosen the foolish things of the world to confound the wise; and God hath chosen the weak things of the world to confound the things which are mighty" (I Corinthians 1:27). I said, "Lord, if you can use my weakness, I am willing."

Then it became very clear to me. If God had the power to bring us through the most dangerous places, often sending angels to help us, surely with the guidance of the Holy Spirit I would be able to write. By faith I grabbed my pencil and started to write.

Little did I realize how hard it would be for me to live through the whole tragedy again. I shed many tears while writing, but the Comforter, the Holy Spirit, urged me to keep on, and the presence of the Lord was very near.

I am unable to explain the thankfulness I felt toward my heavenly Father while I was writing. Very prayerfully I set down every line, and as memories came back to me, even the most tragic ones, my soul was richly blessed. I have learned and experienced that our heavenly Father is mindful of His children, and that in things great or small, He provides for us.

You will find in the following pages miracle after miracle that have been answers to prayer. In situations where we could not expect any help except from our heavenly Father, He always most wonderfully found a way to bring us through.

Perhaps some of you have never had hardships, and you may wonder what you would do if some should come. Or maybe some of you are burdened with problems and don't know where to turn. It is my desire and prayer that this book will be of help to you.

This story of my life actually happened the way I have written it. I have promised the Lord many times that I will be very careful and never take any personal credit for the work of this book. All glory and honor belong to my heavenly Father.

What the Lord has done for me, I am sure He can do for every one of you.

May I take the liberty to ask you, when you read this book, to be willing to forget about your own earthly possessions? Go with me on a journey I had to take. And I pray this book will be a blessing to you.

—The Author

TABLE OF CONTENTS

I

A CHANGED PRAYER MADE THE DIFFERENCE

"Lilli, why are you crying?" Papa asked me.

I looked up, startled. Had my father seen my tears again? Did I myself know why I was crying? I, a teenager, daughter of good parents who were concerned about the happiness and welfare of their children? Did I have any real reason for crying?

A flash review of my life made me wonder. I was born into a Christian home, headed by a godly minister. Our family numbered six: Father, Mother, older sister Marie, Lilli (the writer), Ida, and younger brother, Fritz.

Papa always had a great love for people. He wanted them to know Jesus as their personal Saviour. It gave him much joy to tell others, in church or elsewhere, about Christ. I can well remember hearing him say that he was willing to give his life for the cause of Christ.

As a minister, choir director, and youth leader, Papa was well liked and highly respected.

As soon as we children became old enough to memorize a prayer, we were taught to pray. We had family worship every morning.

We sang a song, Papa read from the Bible, and we all knelt to pray. Papa prayed first, Mother next, then we children, from the oldest to the youngest.

Learning was easy for me and I enjoyed every minute I spent in school. I made good grades and had many friends. Those friends were chosen carefully, because our parents kept strict, godly watch over us children.

Still, in some ways, I led a rather lonely life. We lived in a small town where there were few Christian young people. My parents did not approve of my going out among young people who were not Christians. When I was invited, I usually said I could not accept.

These gatherings were not wild parties or drinking bouts. The young people in those groups were fine folks. Our social activities were playing games and singing songs. The young folks, however, were not Christians, and neither was I. For some reason I felt very uneasy when I was with them, and I did not really enjoy their company. Usually I was sorry afterward that I had gone. I could not understand this. When at the same time some of my friends told me what a wonderful time they had, I could not understand this either. I knew, however, that my parents were praying for me, and I felt those prayers following me everywhere I went.

Is that why I was crying? Because I had received another invitation and did not want to hurt Papa by asking his permission to accept? Yes, that was the reason, and I finally told him so.

I saw both hurt and compassion on his face as he answered, "You have not asked me yet. You may go this time."

I knew my parents were praying that I would give my life to Jesus. Papa had told me over and over that if I would ask Jesus to come into my heart I would then have real joy—the kind of joy I could have only after receiving forgiveness for my sins.

One morning during family devotions when my turn came to pray I said my memorized prayer, as usual. Then suddenly my heart felt broken, and I began to cry. I had a deep desire to pray using my own words, but no words came. I could not understand what made me feel so sinful, more so than ever before in all my seventeen years.

This went on each morning for some time. Always I felt the desire to pray but had no words of my own.

All my life I had been repeating my memorized prayers, listening to my parents' prayers, hearing the Bible read, and joining in the beautiful Gospel singing. My parents had tried to raise me the right way. Shouldn't I have been a Christian by now? Shouldn't I have been ready for heaven?

No, going through all these things did not satisfy the longing in my heart. I was a lost sinner and needed to ask Jesus to come into my heart. Those memorized prayers, beautiful as they might have been, were not my words and did not answer my needs. Jesus wanted me to come to Him just as I was and tell Him my needs with my own words. Poor as they might sound, I needed to say them.

Jesus knew the desire of my heart. One night a group of Christians had gathered in our home for a prayer meeting. After Papa preached a moving sermon, we all knelt to pray. For the first time in my life I found myself praying in my own words, asking Jesus to come into my heart.

The Bible says, "That if thou shalt confess with thy mouth the Lord Jesus, and shalt believe in thine heart that God hath raised him from the dead, thou shalt be saved" (Romans 10:9).

Hebrews 11:6 says further, "He that cometh to God must believe that he is, and that he is a rewarder of them that diligently seek him."

There was great rejoicing in our prayer meeting that night. Many people had been praying for me. Now I, the lost sheep, had come to the fold.

There was great rejoicing in heaven also. "I say unto you, that likewise joy shall be in heaven over one sinner that repenteth, more than over ninety and nine just persons, which need no repentance" (Luke 15:7).

Jesus had been tenderly calling me, and the Holy Spirit had been drawing me. The Bible says no man can come to repentance unless he is drawn by the Holy Spirit. A changed prayer had made the difference. My eyes were opened and I saw everything in a different light after I asked Jesus in my own words to come into my heart and forgive all my sins. I became a new creature in Christ Jesus. "Therefore if any man be in Christ, he is a new creature: old things are passed away; behold, all things are become new" (II Corinthians 5:17).

I had tried to find joy in the things of the world. I could not find it. But that evening I found a new life in Christ. And I found joy as well.

After I accepted Jesus as my Saviour, Papa never again found me crying. I no longer had any desire to go to those non-Christian social gatherings. When I refused the invitations of the young people, they felt sorry for me, thinking I had to stay home. I could answer them, "Oh, no, please don't feel sorry for me any more. I am very happy now. My life has been changed. I found Jesus and He gave me a brand new life and a desire to please Him."

Our family worship became a real blessing to me. What a difference now! Why had I waited so long? Perhaps because I had always thought I was not so bad a person and had seen no reason to change.

Reader, if you have never been born again as the Bible teaches, maybe you are praying a memorized prayer as I did. It did not help me. I was a miserable, lost sinner until I asked

Jesus with my own words to come into my heart.

People saw the change in my life. I could witness to them what Jesus had done for me. He had given me peace and joy that I had never known before.

Our Christian group grew. More young people accepted the Lord and joined our choir. Among them was my sister Ida. When Fritz made his decision for Christ, all our family were Christians except Marie, the oldest, now married and gone from home. As a happy family, we now had one desire and one bond of love—that we might live our lives to please our heavenly Father.

Some time later, on a beautiful Sunday afternoon, 32 of us new believers, dressed in white, lined up by twos near our church, and walked to the river to be baptized. The stream cut through a beautiful valley surrounded by trees and mountains. When we reached the river we walked down steps which had been cut into the bank of the river. A choir sang, "Who Are They That Are Clothed in White?" (words based on Revelation 7:9).

After baptism we returned to the church to join the congregation for the remainder of the service—a sermon, prayer, and communion. The sermon gave helpful instruction to us new members of the church. At the end of the sermon, we 32 knelt around the altar, and the pastor laid his hands on each of us in turn and prayed. Then he gave each of us a verse of

Scripture to use as a guide in life. Communion followed, bringing the blessed service to a close.

That entire afternoon ceremony was a precious experience which I will never forget. I am still thanking God for the changed prayer that brought it all about—the prayer I prayed in my own words instead of memorized words.

II

THE NAZI REGIME

Many books have been written about Hitler and the Nazi regime, exposing the hatred and strife. It is not my desire to emphasize the hatred I saw in the war. Everyone already knows a war brings tragedy and heartaches. It is my desire to report the Lord's marvelous acts of deliverance toward me and my family and other Christians. I know from experience that God is able to do anything we ask Him to do, if it is according to His will. I also know that some people go through trials and suffering without knowing the peace a person can have by turning to God. I want this account to witness to any such readers, as well as to those who know victory in Christ.

Hitler hated the Jews and tried to get rid of them. He even hated Jewish names. Because he considered the Bible Jewish, he asked people with Biblical names to change them. Our parents had given two of us children names from the Bible. Mine was Leah which I changed to Lilli. Rachel, just younger than I, renamed herself Ida.

Because of the extensive German military activity, all the younger men who were physically able were drafted into the army or conscripted for whatever work the government considered important.

I was at work when Papa was commanded to go. On my arrival home, Ida met me at the door and said, "Our papa is not home any more."

Papa gone? My papa, whom I loved so very much? In dazed shock I looked at Mother and said, "Please tell me about his last minutes at home."

Mother answered, "When Papa was ready to leave the house, I handed him a cup of tea. Very broken-hearted, he said, 'I cannot eat or drink. I want to spend the last few minutes with my family in prayer.' We all gathered together for prayer. Very desperately Papa prayed for each one of us, calling us all by name, asking God to take us by the hand and bring us through. Then he said good-by and left."

There were many tears from the whole family as Mother told me this.

Though I had been absent at his departure, it seemed to me I could hear Papa's last prayers. They, along with our own, became our source of strength in the uncertainty around us. We thanked God for the privilege of prayer, and we knew our Heavenly Father was leading the way. Whatever our future might bring, we were safe in the arms of Jesus. If we should be killed through war, a mansion in heaven would await us. My own prayer was:

"Please, Jesus, stay close beside me;
Through the storm You can hide me;
Lead me, guide me safely to the shore
Where I can rest forevermore."

Under Hitler there was always much fear among the people. No one dared to express his feelings, even to ask what would happen to our beautiful Germany. Even ministers had to be careful with their preaching.

At the funeral service of a little girl, the minister used the Scripture: "But Jesus called them unto him, and said, Suffer little children to come unto me, and forbid them not: for of such is the kingdom of God" (Luke 18:16). Then he added, "It is so sad that many children of today cannot come."

Two teachers attended the funeral service, teacher Elsa and teacher Julia. Teacher Julia was all for Hitler. She went to the Nazis and reported that the minister had spoken against Hitler. Teacher Elsa told me that several days later a Nazi had come rushing into her house, had pointed his finger at her, and had asked very excitedly, "What did the minister say at the funeral service?"

"I was very frightened," Elsa told me. "I really did not know what to say, but the words came to me as from heaven itself, 'I am sure Julia must have misunderstood the minister. I know he did not say it that way.' "

To Elsa's great relief, the Nazi had asked no

further questions, the case was closed, and the minister went free. Surely God gave Elsa the right words to speak. Otherwise the minister would have been taken to the concentration camp, perhaps to die there like thousands of other innocent people.

Our family often talked about Uncle Gottlieb, a brother of our papa. He was too old to go into the army. As far as we knew, he was still at his home in a different part of Germany. He had worked hard on his farm, had a beautiful home, and was hoping someday to take life easier. How nice it would be if our family could be with him and his family!

Then suddenly a letter came from Uncle Gottlieb telling us that they had been forced to leave their home. All they had been able to take with them were two horses and a wagon for their daughter Angelika and family, and two horses and a wagon for Uncle Gottlieb and Aunt Sofie. These they had loaded with the most needed things—bedding, clothing, and food. They had been ordered to go farther into western Germany. Hitler was still hoping to win the war, and he wanted the German people to move to the western part as far as possible.

Several months before this I had visited Uncle Gottlieb. I had seen for myself the comforts and conveniences the family enjoyed. Could it be possible that now they were homeless and poor? What a tragedy! Why war? My heart ached.

We became more frightened day by day. We could hear the shooting as it came closer and closer, and we could see people going about dazed, not knowing what to do. What people had built and worked hard for all their lives was being destroyed in moments. Like flowers that bloom beautifully today but by tomorrow are gone, so earthly possessions were suddenly demolished.

Messages of death began to arrive from the battle front. In our town these came to the mayor and he delivered them to the families.

One afternoon while I was visiting my next-door neighbor, the mayor came in. The family looked at each other in hushed dread, fearing for their Robert and Henry in the army. In a faltering voice, the mayor announced, "Your Robert was killed," and he showed them the letter from the army. The family suffered a terrible shock. I felt so sorry for them. My Papa had been taken too, but our family lived in the hope of his return someday.

Several months later, in January of 1945, I saw the mayor going to that neighbor's house again. I thought, "Oh, no, not Henry this time! Wouldn't that be terrible?" But soon the mayor rushed out of that house and into ours. I knew him very well but was surprised as he entered. Sometime before this he had tried to teach me how to raise my hand to make the Hitler salute. Instead of saying "Good morning," I had been told to say "Heil

Hitler." I just could not do that, but I did not risk saying so or I would have been known as anti-Nazi.

I thought the mayor looked frightened now as he told us in a low voice why he was going from house to house. We all listened in silence. "You are to pack and get ready to escape," he said.

"Escape?" I asked. "How? Where? How are we going to take our things? We do not have any horses."

"Farmers are commanded to give up some of their horses and wagons to those who do not have any," he explained, "and two families have to share one wagon. Hitler wants to move us all farther west. He hopes there we will be safe from the enemy troops.

"Can this really be possible?" I thought. "Or am I dreaming?" Is my country in such a shape that no one dares to say, "I do not want to leave my home?"

It was a command. The Nazis did not ask if we wanted to go. They ordered us to pack and be ready in five hours.

My sister Ida was in training three miles from home, on one of the large farms Hitler used in his training program. All boys and girls were compelled to begin training at the age of sixteen. They were taught at these farms about Hitler first, then about farm work. They were lined up much of the time and had to march to their work to the count of one-two, one-two. Usually there were ten girls or ten boys in a group with a leader, all dressed alike in clothes furnished by the Nazis.

"I hope Ida is still at the farm," Mother said. "It would be too bad if she had to escape alone. Lilli, you must go to the farm and bring her home if she is still there."

I grabbed my coat and started out. The three-mile walk was agony for me for I feared Ida would be gone before I could get there. At last I arrived, looked down the long driveway, and saw Ida standing all alone, waiting for me in front of the building with her little bag of clothing in her hand.

"Lilli!" she screamed almost hysterically, "I am so glad you came. I was so worried you would escape without me."

We threw our arms around each other as tears rolled down our faces.

"How is Mother doing in all this?" Ida asked. "And Brother Fritz?"

"They are holding up as well as can be expected," I answered, "but are very down-hearted about escaping. Thank God we can be together again. Where are all the other girls?"

"They all went home to their families."

"Oh, Ida, we must hurry home to help Mother. In five hours, our mayor told us, our transportation will be at our house for us to load up our belongings."

"I wonder where Hitler is going to take us," Ida said as we started for home. "This is January, and so cold. We probably will freeze to death."

"He wants us to flee to the western part of Germany, farther away from enemy troops, the mayor told us. We are in a very sad situation. And who can help us? But remember, Ida, God will be with us. The Bible says God never leaves nor forsakes those who put their trust in Him, and God's Word is true. What did your leader on the Hitler farm say about escaping?"

"Not much. She looked very frightened to me."

On our arrival at home, Mother was waiting for us, relieved to see both of us. There was joy in our family in spite of tragedy. Now at least we had Ida with us again.

"But Papa! Where is he?" Fritz, only twelve years old, asked with tears in his eyes. "Are we leaving our home? When Papa comes back, he will never find us."

"Fritz, this is war," Mother explained. "All of us are heart-broken. If our Papa could be with us, then everything would be so much better."

We had not heard from Papa since he had left, months before. Like thousands of others, he was a missing man. There are no words to describe the heartaches suffered over missing ones.

"We really have to hurry to get ready," Mother said urgently. "Lilli and Ida, you do the packing. On the shelves are the linen sacks. In them you can pack our bedding and clothing. I will do some baking—rye bread and cookies."

Fritz spoke up. "Mother, I really love my rabbit. What is going to happen to him?"

"Yes, Fritz, it's too bad," Ida sympathized. "But all you can do is give him a lot of feed and hope some kind person will take care of him."

Time went fast. We tried to hurry. When the packing was done, Ida made pancakes and tea. We set the roundtable in the living room for our last meal in our home.

The four of us, deeply touched, gathered around the table. Mother said grace, thanking God for the food. Then she looked at us and asked without expecting an answer, "Where are we going to have our next meal?"

Only God knew.

Our packed things waited on a pile near the door. Soon they, like us, would be pushed out, and taken—where? We felt like wanderers out at sea without a destination. But we knew we had an anchor in Jesus. We knew that He would be our pilot and would steer our ship to some safe harbor.

Our family counted it a great privilege to know Jesus. We knew how to pray. We knelt for the last time in our home and prayed in desperation, our hearts crushed and our faces streaming with tears. Through all our insecurity, we felt a sure connection with our Heavenly Father, and we committed ourselves completely into His hands. We not only knew but also experienced what the

Bible means when it says, "Draw nigh to God, and he will draw nigh to you" (James 4:2).

We heard voices outside. Mother looked out and announced, "Oh children, our transportation is here—a couple of small horses pulling a wagon and a boy driving them."

We had to share the wagon with Marge, our next-door neighbor, and her family. We all loaded our things and prepared to leave.

Before closing the door of our house for the last time, I asked, "Mother, do you have our money with you?"

"Yes, Lilli, I have."

"Wait! wait!" Fritz begged before stepping up into the wagon. "I have to go and say good-by to my rabbit."

As we began our journey, horse-drawn wagons came from everywhere and formed long caravans as far as our eyes could see.

I looked back at our home once more. Would I ever see it again? Then I looked ahead, knowing our Heavenly Father would never leave nor forsake us. The sense of emptiness left me; fulness and peace filled my soul.

So dark to me was the future;
Black clouds hung over the land;
But this one thing I was sure of:
I was led by my Father's hand.
He dresses lilies in the field,
And the little sparrow He feeds;
How much more He loves His children!
I know my Heavenly Father leads.

With Marie gone from home, I was the oldest child in our evacuating family. And since Mother was in poor health, much responsibility fell on me. I had to see that everything was in order. I had to find feed for the horses (the driver should have but didn't). As we drove past farms that, like our home, had been recently vacated, I found hay, corn, and straw in the barns or fields. Most of the time, though, the horses went pitifully hungry because we were not given time to feed them regularly or to let them eat long enough. Always we had to move on and stay in line with the other wagons.

My responsibilities increased as our driver, Max, let his horses lag. Not interested in going farther into western Germany, he grew listless and often went to sleep on the wagon. This caused delay to the line of wagons behind us. On narrow roads I spent much time walking beside the horses, urging them to go faster and to keep up with the wagons ahead. If only Papa could have been with us!

"Will I ever see my papa again?" I often asked myself. "Is he still alive and in good health?"

Mother often voiced our concern aloud. "Will God bring Papa and us together again?" His love was very dear to all of us. How desperately he prayed for us that day before he left home! And how he did love God with all his heart!

Though we knew we might never see Papa

again in this life, we knew we could look forward to meeting him in heaven. And in heaven there would be no parting and no more tears. "For the Lamb which is in the midst of the throne shall feed them, and shall lead them unto living fountains of waters: and God shall wipe away all tears from their eyes" (Revelation 7:17).

With my heart bleeding over the cruelty that war can bring to innocent people, I dedicated this poem to my papa:

Humble and kind was my own father,
　　But war had no mercy. And I say,
With thousands and thousands of others,
　　"O God, why was it that way?"
My father truly loved Jesus,
　　And loved to show others the way.
When will we meet him in heaven
　　And know the reason why?
My heart is ready to break
　　While writing this poem, but yet
I think he's in heaven by now,
　　Waiting for me at the gate.
There will be no more tears
　　Or griefs on that beautiful shore;
And together we will sing
　　God's praises for evermore.

Desolated, we traveled almost day and night. There were no restaurants or coffee shops. Roads were crowded with German soldiers and with thousands of people seeking to escape.

Perhaps you are wondering, "Where did these people clean up? Did they have any privacy for bathing or changing clothes? What did they eat?"

In all those crowds of people, I can truthfully say I never once heard anyone complain about wanting a bath, a good meal, or a soft bed. Such things were not uppermost in our minds. We were running for our lives. Dangers faced us everywhere. The terrors of war were all around us. War planes zoomed low, shooting and killing people and horses. We ate once or twice a day from the food we had packed before we left home. Sometimes we found potatoes or other food at night in the empty houses along the way. Then we cooked and ate meals, using cookware and dishes we had with us. If we found water we were happy to clean up, but we were not so concerned with how we looked on the outside. We were more concerned with how we looked to the Lord, for we wanted to trust Him, depending on Him and keeping ourselves ready to meet Him at any moment.

When Marge and her three small children were loaded on our wagon at the time we left home, there was no room for Marge's mother Ema. She was told to go on the nearest neighbor's wagon with some of her luggage. Those neighbors promised to drive right behind us so we would be together. But somehow in the rush and confusion they must have taken a different road. That first night when

Marge looked for the food she had packed for her family, she realized it was all with her mother Ema. We tried our best to find Ema but had to give up. There were too many people and there was too much danger of being separated if we walked very far from our wagon.

Marge and her children had nothing to eat. It was heart-breaking to listen to the cries of her hungry children. Her husband was in the army. She had not heard from him for months. Perhaps he was killed. Now she and the children were on the street without food. No Nazis came around asking if a woman needed help.

"What has happened to our powerful Germany?" I asked myself.

Snow lay on the ground. We shivered with cold. Close to the road we saw an empty house. We stopped there a short time. Thankfully I found some wood and a stove. I made a fire and we prepared hot tea. Mother took out a loaf of our rye bread. We had some jam and butter that we had saved from our ration-card allowance. Mother took a large knife and cut slices from that loaf. We shared our food with Marge and her children as much as we could.

"Does my rabbit have something to eat also?" Fritz wondered while we ate.

"I am sure someone has fed him," Ida told him.

After eating we went back to our wagon to continue our journey with the other horses and wagons.

But we were shocked and frightened to see much blood on the road, and overturned wagons in the snowy fields. How could wagons get into the fields, across deep ditches on both sides of the road?

"Lilli!" Mother exclaimed, "Go and ask what happened."

Would I get an answer? We were not supposed to know what was going on. We were always told Hitler was going to win the war.

I took courage and asked some of the refugees. They said enemy war planes had just gone over, swooping low, shooting people and horses.

My heart overflowed with thankfulness to God for His protection to our family and Marge's. I thought, "The Lord truly brought us through, like the children of Israel through the Red Sea. If we had not stopped to make hot tea, we would have been in that spot where the planes came down. Some or all of us may have been killed. Surely 'the eye of the Lord is upon them that fear him . . .' (Psalm 33:18). 'Are not five sparrows sold for two farthings, and not one of them is forgotten before God? But even the very hairs of your head are all numbered. Fear not therefore: ye are of more value than many sparrows' " (Luke 12:6, 7).

There was a constant prayer in my heart, not for a meal or for a night in a soft bed; I just asked the Lord to watch over us and keep us safe. At night we were especially frightened. There were no street lights. Behind us we could see buildings on fire, probably started by the hand grenades of the soldiers. People were screaming, children were crying, but nobody ever stopped or tried to help. No wonder, if all mayors told their evacuating people what ours had told us. Our mayor had given us a speech, saying, "The caravan must keep moving. All must get away as fast as possible. Many of the drivers must be women, as the government does not furnish men drivers for families that have their own horses and wagons. There will be few men drivers, because men are in the army. This means if a woman driver's wagon breaks down, the other wagons must move on without that one. Perhaps help will come later, but there must be no interruptions."

I thought that was very cruel. How could a lady get help if no one was permitted to help her? Believe me, it was heartbreaking to see the suffering on the roads.

Most of the fleeing people around us were not Christians. Plainly, they did not have the peace of Jesus in their hearts. In a time like that it meant everything to have a caring Father in heaven. We found comfort in these words from Jesus: "These things have I spoken unto you, that in me ye might have peace. In the world ye shall have tribulation: but be of good cheer; I have overcome the world" (John 16:33). Such promises spoke to us loudly. We knew the strength we had was not ours but God's.

The way became long. Life turned into a nightmare. What was ahead? People did not mention the future to each other. Even we as a family seldom did. Mother would often repeat, "If Papa could be with us, then everything would be so much better."

Marge grew discouraged and physically weak. Frequently she would say, "If only I could find my mother again."

Often Mother asked if we were hungry. By now we had only one loaf of bread and some butter left. "After that is gone, then what?" was her question. It would be hard to see little Fritz completely without food.

When Moses led the children of Israel through the wilderness, God sent them bread from heaven, enough for each day. "Then said the Lord unto Moses, Behold, I will rain bread from heaven for you; and the people shall go out and gather a certain rate every day" (Exodus 16:4). We had the same God. After our last loaf of bread was gone, God did supply for us and He kept us from starving. Though sometimes we did not have much to eat, we never suffered severe hunger or thirst. And each day He gave us new strength.

> I truly can say
> That day by day
> Our Heavenly Father led us.
> In His strength we did survive.

With His heavenly manna
He did feed us
With His watchful eye
He did keep us.

With His strong hand
He did hold us.
Only through Him we conquered-.
His name is Jesus, Jesus, Jesus.

We kept searching for Ema, but our search
was fruitless among the crowds. The fear grew
worse and worse. People tried to get away
faster and faster. Some families began pushing their wagons because their poorly-fed
horses were no longer strong enough to pull
them alone. The desperation grew beyond
description.

One day I noticed two girls walking beside
the caravans, dressed as Ida had dressed
when she was on the Nazi farm. I said, "Look,
Ida. Do you know those girls?"

Ida looked. "Oh, yes! It is Ani and Heidi.
We were together in training on the Hitler
farm."

Springing from the wagon to greet the girls,
Ida called, "Ani, are you all alone? Where is
your family? And Heidi? Are you alone also?"

With tears streaming down their faces, the
girls said, "It took us too many hours to get
home from the Hitler farm. When we arrived,
our families had already left. We could not
find them. Now we are on the road without

any food or bedding."

My heart ached for them.

> Sometimes I didn't understand
> My Father's leading hand;
> But no one else could help me,
> And I went to prayer on my knees.
> "Please, Father, hear my plea."

> He heard, and His arms went
>   around me.
>   He whispered, "My child, I am
>   with thee;
> Just have faith and trust in me;
> I have promised to see you through.
> And you know My Word is true."

In our travels, I was hoping we might find Uncle Gottlieb and his family among the crowds. Surely we could help each other if we could be together. And in my heart I repeated with Mother, "If only Papa could be with us."

Suddenly we saw enemy soldiers in front of us. For several minutes there was complete silence among our crowds. Then some spoke up saying, "This is what Hitler did to us. Why couldn't we stay in our homes?" Some said, "Hitler tried to win the war without God."

III

BULLETS DROPPED
AROUND US

Hardly had the enemy soldiers appeared in front of us when the German soldiers met them, and the battle was on.

The roads were packed with frightened refugees. I noticed one refugee standing with his hat off and his eyes raised upward. "Is he ready for heaven?" I wondered.

Our family looked for a place to hide. Marge chose to stay on the wagon. Seeing a large tree, we hurried to it. I lifted my eyes toward heaven and from my innermost being I cried out, "Lord, here we are. Please help us."

I know my prayer was heard. I felt the presence of God and His angels as the bullets dropped around us without hitting us.

Being directed to a certain building for the night, we crowded in among those already there and sat on the floor. In the next room lay a dead woman. During the night a wounded German soldier was brought in, shot in the knee. He pleaded with us not to leave him there. We knew, however, that we would be moving on day after day, and we were unable to help him in any way. I often wondered what happened to him. He probably was shot, like thousands of others.

By morning we were very thirsty. Marge's children especially needed drinks. I saw a house about 200 feet from the one we were in. The owners had fled and the house was being used by refugees. I went in and made hot tea. As I went to leave, a soldier threw a hand grenade into the house. A terrible explosion followed and in minutes the house was in flames. Pale and frightened, I stumbled back to my family with the tea.

"Lilli, what happened?" Mother wanted to know.

Trembling all over, I tried to tell them.

"Did anyone get hurt?" Fritz asked.

"Yes, nine people were killed, and their families were crying and screaming. I barely got out myself."

"Surely God watched over you," Ida said.

"Yes," I emphasized, "every step of the way. The Bible says, 'For he shall give his angels charge over thee, to keep thee in all thy ways. They shall bear thee up in their hands, lest thou dash thy foot against a stone' " (Psalm 91:11, 12).

I wish I could express myself so that every reader could have the awareness of the Almighty hand of God as we did. He is ruler of heaven and earth, King of kings, and Lord of lords; yet He cares for you and me and gives

His angels charge over us. In all the suffering, there was praise in my heart that I could call the Lord Jesus my Saviour, and that He loved my family and me so much.

As we looked around that morning, we saw German uniforms piled in heaps but not a single German soldier in sight. The enemy soldiers were dancing in the street for joy, celebrating the victory.

What did those heaps of German uniforms mean? According to some whisperings, the German soldiers who had worn those uniforms had changed into civilian clothes and sneaked away.

For a few moments, my thoughts turned to the unanswerable questions of war. Why did we have to have war? War separated families. War sent people from their homes and put them on the street. War took millions of lives. War brought destruction. Where was Papa? Where was Marie? Was she forced to escape, and suffer on the way? Where was Uncle Gottlieb and his family?

The crowds of refugees milling around brought me back to our situation. We had to go on, for we couldn't stay here. We needed a place to live. That evening we stopped as usual at a house whose owners had escaped. Others stopped there too, making twenty-six in all. Two soldiers came in, looked us over, and left saying they would be back later.

We were a roomful of frightened women and children. We hoped they might not return. But one hour later, near midnight, they did return, one of them in great anger.

We looked at the soldiers in helpless terror, unable to hide or flee. They told us through the few who could understand the language that they would kill us before the night was over. We watched them count us and then count the number of bullets they would need. The room grew deathly quiet, but many of us were praying. After a while the angry soldier commanded the other one to shoot all twenty-six of us. Mother asked through the interpreters if our family could sing a song and pray together before we would be killed. The soldier gave permission. We joined hands in our sitting position on the floor, and Mother began to pray aloud. Almost right away he yelled at her to be quiet because she prayed in German, which he could not understand. Mother stopped praying aloud, but we kept on praying silently.

I shall never forget that experience. The room seemed to be filled with angels. "The angel of the Lord encampeth round about them that fear him, and delivereth them" (Psalm 34:7). Heaven seemed close. The guns were loaded, the triggers were waiting to be pulled, and we were ready for heaven. We could say with Stephen as he was being stoned, "Behold, I see the heavens opened, and the Son of man standing on the right hand of God" (Acts 7:56). I now can understand how Isaac must have felt as he lay on the altar waiting for his father Abraham to use him as an offering.

Fear left us, and we whispered comforting words to each other. "And the Lord, he is is that doth go before thee; he will be with thee, he will not fail thee, neither forsake thee: fear not, neither be dismayed" (Deuteromony 31:8).

The night wore on. Perhaps feeling that too much time was being lost, the angry soldier told the other soldier, "If you do not carry out my order, I will shoot you."

Plainly, the soldier spoken to did not know what to do. He acted bewildered. He took out his billfold and opened it to pictures of his mother, his wife, and his children. He looked at them, called them by name, and began to sob, "Why are you all so far away from me? Why can't we be together? Why do I have to kill all these people? They have done nothing wrong to me."

He cried so loudly that other soldiers on the street heard him and came rushing in to find out what was going on. They questioned both soldiers' right to be there and took them out. We knew God had kept that soldier from carrying out the order to kill us, and we thanked Him for deliverance.

Daylight came. We began looking through the house for food. Though we were not hungry after the horror of the night, we knew our bodies needed nourishment and strength for the day. We found some potatoes and made a

41

big kettle of potato soup for all 26 of us.

As we left that house, Mother said, "I wonder how I would have felt last night if I had not been able to pray and receive assurance of the Lord's presence. We were only one breath away from eternity."

"I never knew before," I answered, "that the Lord can fill a heart with such wonderful peace as He did while we sat there on the floor waiting and praying, and wondering what He had in mind for us. If He wanted to take us home I was ready; if not, I promised Him I would praise Him and tell others about it."

That evening we had great difficulty finding a place to stay over night, and finding feed for our horses. Our driver had left us and had gone home to his family, for there was no German government to hire him any longer. The weather had turned very cold and a snowstorm had set in.

I went back to talk things over with Frieda, the lady behind us. She said, "My baby died today, I still have it on the wagon. I don't know where or how to bury it since the ground is frozen."

How could I help her? How could I comfort her? I put my arms around her and wept with her.

A soldier came by, asking if he could help us. Frieda was able to speak to him. She told him we needed a room for the night and feed for the horses.

"Come with me," he told us, "and I will

help you."

That soldier kept on walking in the darkness, and we did not know any better than to follow him. I felt serious misgivings, even fear, as we entered an unlighted building. I thought, "Can there be feed for horses in this building?"

I became even more frightened while following him down a long, dark hall. Suddenly a door opened and a soldier faced me. I looked for Frieda. She was gone. My heart cried out with everything that was in me, "Oh, my God, what will happen to me now? If he kills me here, my family will never find out what happened to me. Jesus, please help me."

That soldier did not touch me. God must have put a hedge around me like the one He put around Job. I have heard many people talk about their guardian angel. I know I was brought out of that building by my guardian angel, and directed to my family. I could never have found my way back by myself, bewildered as I was in the darkness. When I got back I was trembling from the fear and the cold, like a leaf blown by the wind.

Providentially, our family found a little room where we could stay. What happened to Frieda and her dead baby I will never know.

Mother made us some hot soup for supper, but I could not eat. I was still shaking all over from my frightful experience. Supper was not important. Thankfulness was. All of us thanked the Lord that I was still alive and with my family.

We found no feed for our horses, but we did find a little room at one end of the building where they could be sheltered. Since the horses had to bend their bodies around a curve to get into such tiny quarters, I backed them in. This way they could not see, and so did not balk.

Next morning when we went outside we found our wagon covered with snow, our valuable things missing, and our other things scattered in the snow.

Heart-broken, we gathered our pitifully few things together and reloaded them. Then I tried to get the horses out from their cramped quarters. This time I had to lead them head first, for there was not enough room to turn them around in their tiny shelter. I had great difficulty making them bend themselves, especially now that they could see their predicament. Instinctively cautious, they held back. Once more, in my time of desperate need, God made impossible things possible, and the horses finally came out.

After a scanty breakfast we got on our way, feeling carried by the power of God.

It is often true that people in great fear don't like to talk. As for me, in my times of greatest fear, I did my talking silently—in prayer. I know my family did also. That close contact with the Lord gave us new strength for every need.

Our need for strength was constant. As we

moved along through the middle of what had just been battlefields and fighting zones, the horrors of war almost overwhelmed us. We saw dead bodies sticking out of the snow lining the roads. Mother looked at me grief-stricken and said, "Maybe the body of our dear papa is lying around somewhere on the streets or in the fields."

Ida added sadly, "It would be so wonderful to be in our own home again, in a warm room, with Papa among us. We could sing and play our instruments. Instead we are wandering in the cold, without food and with nowhere to go."

"Yes, I would like to be home with my rabbit," Fritz reminded all of us. "I hope he is still alive."

One afternoon we were about to enter a building to seek shelter for the night when we were stopped by a friendly woman. She warned us against entering there and directed us to another building. Later we learned that in the first building young people had been taken from their refugee parents and kept to be put to work, cleaning up the dead bodies from the streets and fields and dumping them into mass graves that had been war trenches.

That night, while we slept, the horses that the German government had furnished us for our escape were taken. There we were, stranded with other refugees in that house.

As usual on farms whose owners had escaped, there was some food. In this case it was mostly potatoes, so we ate potatoes three times a day.

Several weeks went by. The potato supply got low. We knew we could not stay much longer here. What should we do? We could not return to our own homes. Where could we go?

My family and I grew desperate. "What shall we do?" Mother moaned. "Which way shall we turn?"

After praying earnestly, we felt God wanted us to pack as many of our things as we could carry and start out walking.

Fritz was only 12 years old, and Mother was in poor health. Neither of them could carry much. That left most of the load with Ida and me.

We had to leave all bedding except one comforter and one pillow. Also we had to leave all except the few most needed dishes. Fritz carried the bucket of butter we had saved from ration card allowances, and hoisted a bag of some clothing on his back. Ida took a small sack of flour and some dishes. I shouldered the comforter and some other needed things. Mother took the pillow and her handbag. We hoped soon we could find jobs and a place to live.

Marge, the lady who had ridden with us on our wagon, was not able to walk with us. Her children were too small, and she herself was not well. We said good-by to them and promised if we found her mother Ema, we would help bring her back.

We put ourselves in the hands of the Lord and started out. With few earthly possessions to depend on, we took comfort in knowing we had a rich Father in heaven. This Father says, "Therefore take no thought, saying, What shall we eat? or, What shall we drink? or, Wherewithal shall we be clothed . . .? For your heavenly Father knoweth that ye have need of all these things" (Matthew 6:31, 32).

By now it was April of 1945, just three months after we began our flight from home. What long months they had been! What miles we had covered! What horrors we had been through!

Ten minutes of walking brought us a glad surprise. We met Ema, trudging along the rough road. All she owned was the walking stick in her hand.

Ema had a little boy with her. We soon recognized him as Benny, who had lived with his family down the street from us. His mother had been very ill at the time of the escape. His father had been taken into the army, and the children had had to care for her the best they could. They had made a bed for her on the wagon. Then, because it was too crowded for all of them, nine-year-old Benny was sent with Ema. The two soon lost sight of his family and still had not found them.

"What a heart-breaking sight!" I thought as I looked at them—an old, worn-out woman with nothing in this world but a cane, and a

47

helpless little boy with a small bag containing several ears of dry corn.

Ema said, "When he gets too hungry, he eats a little of that corn."

We told Ema about her daughter Marge, and showed her the building where we had left the family. She thanked us through tears, said good-by to us, and hurried toward the building, taking little Benny with her. We have never seen them since.

"I'm sure they will have a happy reunion," Ida remarked.

All of us felt that way too, thankful that we could have a part in getting them together. "If only Benny's family could have been there too!" I said.

Several hours later another glad surprise came to us. We saw Linda and her little brother Hans on the street. I had known Linda before the escape. Remembering she had often told me about her sick mother, I asked her, "Where is your mother?"

Linda wept. "While we were on the road, my mother died. We didn't know what to do with her body, and no one stopped to help us. Everyone was in too much of a hurry. It so happened that we passed a little church. Prayerfully, we laid the body of our dear mother in that church, hoping someone would be so kind as to bury her. My father and two brothers had to go to war. Only God knows if we will ever meet again."

Knowing Linda loved Jesus, I put my arms

around her and said, "Jesus will always be with you." And I quoted, " 'The Lord is thy keeper: the Lord is thy shade upon thy right hand. The Lord shall preserve thee from all evil: he shall preserve thy soul' (Psalm 121:5, 7). Just take the hand of Jesus, Linda. He will help you."

"Yes," Linda said, "I know."

We parted in tears and never saw each other again. But I know there will be a meeting place before His glorious throne where saints will gather from the East, the West, the North, and the South. There we will meet.

> We found ourselves all broken-
>   hearted
> In the valley,
> But Jesus was standing by.
>
> To each one He whispered,
> "My child, just trust me;
> I am standing close by your side.
>
> When darkness falls around you,
> And tragedy overwhelms you,
> Fear not; I am standing by.
>
> My eye is watching over you
> So nothing wrong can harm you:
> In the valley, I'm standing by."

Jesus did stand by us. We found Him a very close Friend in every time of need.

One thing we especially longed for was a Bible. Through the escape we had lost all our Bibles and hymnbooks. When we left home, our wagon was crowded, so we had put one suitcase on the wagon with Marge's mother, Ema. All of our Bibles and songbooks were in that suitcase. Now that suitcase was gone.

One day, however, we found a beautiful Bible lying on the road. With tears in her eyes Mother almost shouted, "God is so good!"

"It was lying there just for us," Ida declared.

We stopped and read from that precious Book. And many days thereafter it furnished guidance and comfort when our lives seemed the darkest. That Bible, old and rebound, is still a priceless possession in our family.

Mother's poor health gave me great concern. Frequently I asked her, "Mother, can you walk all right?"

"Yes, Lilli," she assured me. "I am still able to walk."

If she would have become too sick to walk, I don't know what we would have done. There were no doctors to help us.

I saw one mother who had four small children. She could carry only one. Her four-year-old boy had to walk—his little feet soaking wet from the melting snow and mud. He cried nearly all the time and begged his mother not to walk too fast. Sometimes he lagged far behind. My heart ached for him.

Days and miles brought us out of the thick

of the horror and through the bitterness of winter. During the spring and summer we worked for various farmers. Then the government began offering some help to refugees.

In October we moved into the beautiful little town of Lichtenburg. The government gave ten of us families a large room to share together, and placed other families similarly. Each family was given a pile of straw and one bowl of potato soup each day. During the day we shoved the straw together to sit on. At night we spread it out to sleep on. All ten families shared the wood stove in the hall, taking turns cooking what potatoes were available.

There were potatoes in the fields piled in great heaps covered with straw and dirt. The farmers had been forced to give these to the government. Armed soldiers guarded the potatoes. Sometimes a good-hearted soldier would give us some potatoes. We had money and could have bought food in stores, but stores were empty. No one knew what had happened to groceries and merchandise.

I longed to find a job, but little Lichtenburg had no jobs to offer. Although sitting around did not appeal to me, there was little else to do.

Many times while sitting on our straw and talking with each other, our thoughts went to the future.

"Will we see Papa again?" was always uppermost in our minds.

"Where can I find a job?" I often wondered aloud. "It is a little difficult to live without knowing the future." We knew the Lord would take care of us, but the Bible says "that if any would not work, neither should he eat" (II Thessalonians 3:10).

"I keep thinking about Ani and Heidi," Ida would say over and over. "Do you remember them, Mother? The two girls we found walking on the street? The two that I had lived with on the Hitler youth farm? I wonder whether they ever found their families."

Mother usually added consolingly, "Yes, Ida, we have much to be thankful for. Even though it is hard that Papa cannot be with us, at least the rest of us are together.

Refugee life became very depressing at times, but my family and I could look to Jesus. Many were without Him. Bitterness hung over them like a dark cloud that never let the sun shine through. Often we heard them say, "If there is a God of love, how can He let this happen to our beautiful Germany?" They did not seem to recognize the sin and cruelty of the Nazi regime. Of course, most of us German people did not know much of what the Nazis had done.

Even when the war ended, its desolation went on. Stores could not find any merchandise to sell to the people who were in need. And many people died of starvation, especially older refugees who were separated from their children. We saw them sitting in corners in the same building where we were, lice crawling on their clothes. It was hard to believe. Not one person came to take these old people in or even to clean them up.

"Is there any hope for a better future?" Mother often wondered.

After weeks of sleeping and sitting on piles of straw, our ten families were given five rooms in a beach hotel. The rooms were small, and two families had to share each one. Again there was no furniture, and this time there was not even any straw. Because there was no furniture in the stores for us to buy, we didn't know what to do.

Then we found two beds outdoors. Though the mattresses were soaked from months of rain, and though we knew it was unhealthful to sleep on wet mattresses, we gratefully brought them in and used them. Gradually they dried, much to our satisfaction and comfort.

Because we did not have a church, we came together in our rooms for prayer meetings. Here we read the Bible, sang hymns, and prayed. Women, young children, and a few old men made up our group. Young and middle-aged men were missing or dead.

Those were desperate prayers with many tears. We loved the Lord, and we trusted Him to see us through. Still in the flesh, however, we felt crushed. We found comfort in verses such as: "When thou passest through the waters, I will be with thee; and through the rivers, they shall not overflow thee; when thou walkest through the fire, thou shalt not be burned; neither shall the flame kindle upon thee" (Isaiah 43:2). Our requests were not for riches or fame but for the Lord's presence and direction.

Fritz and the other eleven-to-thirteen-year-old boys among us had their own prayer meetings in a room next to ours. They read Scriptures and prayed so earnestly and loudly that we sometimes heard them in our room where we were meeting. A revival took place among them, and several of them were saved.

Those were never-to-be-forgotten prayer meetings. We had experienced poverty in earthly things; now God helped us grow rich in spiritual things. He gave us a revival, refreshed our souls, and filled our hearts with joy.

My words are too few to bring out the gratefulness and praise I felt for God's nearness and protection during those terrible months. He kept our bodies fed in the midst of starvation; He gave us physical strength for seeming impossibilities; He revived our souls; and He preserved us from harm when the bullets dropped around us. I know the Bible is true.

"And, behold, I am with thee, and will keep thee in all places whither thou goest, . . . I will not leave thee . . ." (Genesis 28:15).

IV

A MIRACLE

"Lilli," Mother suggested, "I feel you should write to Aunt Frederika to find out if her family is still alive, and if she still lives in her own home. If she receives your letter, maybe she could tell us where Uncle Gottlieb and his family are. All we know about them is that they had to escape."

Aunt Frederika's husband was no longer living. He had been a brother to our papa and to Uncle Gottlieb. We had lost her address, but I remembered it correctly and wrote.

We could hardly believe our eyes when, a week later, we received a letter from Uncle Gottlieb.

"How marvelous! I am so happy we tried," Mother said, tearing open the envelope and reading. "The whole family is still alive. Uncle Gottlieb does not live very far from Aunt Frederika. She told him about our letter."

This gave us a little encouragement. Maybe we could see each other again sometime.

I wondered how Uncle Gottlieb and his family must feel now about their new type of living. I remembered what a beautiful, well-furnished farm home they had enjoyed in a lovely part of eastern Germany before they were forced to leave.

Several months went by. Autumn cooled into winter, and we were thankful for our hotel room in Lichtenburg. We were also thankful we were still able to get some potatoes from the fields that belonged to the government. But there were no jobs to find. For this we were very sad.

One day, in March of 1946, very unexpectedly, the main office of the government in that area called for a representative from each refugee family. That meant girls because there were no men among us.

As we girls did that 16-kilometer (10-mile) walk to Felsenthal, we kept wondering why we were to appear in that office. We all knew the Lord as our Saviour, and a number of times we stopped for prayer. We needed new strength, and we needed understanding. Very exhausted, we finally arrived in Felsenthal, hoping the call might be to offer us jobs.

The government official told us to go home and get our families ready to move to Russia, most likely Siberia, where people were needed the most. "You should be working," he said. "We don't have jobs for you here, and you are needed for work there."

Speechless with shock and despair, we looked at him hopelessly, then turned and stumbled toward the door.

On our way home we prayed helplessly, "Please, Jesus, perform a miracle." We felt that being sent to Siberia would be the worst thing that could happen to anybody. We had heard that in Russia criminals were sent to Siberia.

We almost broke down. The burden seemed more than we could bear: first had been the fear during the war; next, the forced escape and the giving up of our homes; then further loss of our possessions along the way. There had been the pain of family separations. Now this. My own thoughts kept going to Papa. Where is he? Can he be alive? And Marie? With no information available for finding out about missing family members, when will we ever learn about either of them?

Late that evening, with weary feet and heavy hearts, we finished those long ten miles home. Our families were anxiously waiting for us.

"What did the officer tell you?" Mother asked at once.

"Oh, Mother, we have to get ready for a trip to Russia. Most likely it will be Siberia, the officer said. That was the reason they called us."

My family was shocked with me. Mother said hopelessly, "Not all of us will reach Siberia. We probably will die of starvation or freeze to death."

Ida made a wishful suggestion. "Maybe we could find another place to live."

Our family shared our room with a lady named Anna and her two children. Anna had an older daughter, Susie, who like our Ida had been in training on a Nazi youth farm. Susie, like Ani and Heidi, had had too far to go home in the allotted five hours. She had had to escape alone, like thousands of other boys and girls, most of them never to see their families again. Hearing the new prospect of Siberia, Anna was heart-broken.

"I never will see my daughter again," she kept saying, "and my husband Rudolf. I lost him through the war, too."

We prayed desperately. My family and I had been so wonderfully led by the Father's hand this far. Surely He would not take His hand away from us now.

Several days later we found out through a German farmer that it was not the government's idea to have us move. The German people in Lichtenburg were trying to get us out of their beach hotels. By summertime they could use their hotels for paying guests. Since there were no jobs for us in Lichtenburg, these German hotel owners had gone to the government officials and had bribed them to transport us.

It is hard to believe that one German would do something like that to another German, but money counts—at least it did in that little town.

A week went by. Everything was quiet. We came together in our rooms for prayer. We needed strength which no human could give us. We began to hope the government had forgotten to transport us.

Erna, in the room next to ours, said, "I wish I could take my children and hide in the woods, but it is too snowy and cold."

I thought of Uncle Gottlieb. He too had been forced to escape. Maybe he would come and help us out of this town.

We soon learned that the government officials had not forgotten. One of them came with the mayor of Lichtenburg to our hotel. They went from door to door, telling us to be ready in several hours.

"Can this be possible?" I thought, almost unable to speak. "To Siberia?"

We looked at each other helplessly, compassionately, deeply moved.

I said to the mayor, "It is 16 kilometers to the train depot. How are we going to get there?"

He replied, "Farmers are commanded to furnish you transportation."

It took all our strength to pack our few belongings.

When I saw horse-drawn wagons coming down the street I still could not believe we were actually going. Questions came to my mind again and again. Do we have to go to Siberia? Is it really not possible to find jobs here?

Lisi, a friend, and I were told by the mayor to go to the bakery and get bread for the people.

"How much bread are we to get?" Lisi asked.

"Ten loaves. Here is a basket and here is a piece of paper telling how much they should give you."

"Mr. Mayor," I interrupted, "ten loaves for forty people?"

"Yes," he answered with raised voice, "That is all we can give you, one-fourth of a loaf per person."

By now the ten families had gathered outside in front of the hotel. I saw some beginning to cry. I heard some say, "We will die of starvation."

But we were helpless. We were ordered by the government. We had to obey.

Lisi and I started for the bakery, almost too weak to walk. I stopped to pray, took a few steps, stopped to pray again, took a few steps, and so on. I don't know how many times I stopped to pray, but I do know I prayed. "Please, Lord, help us. Lord Jesus, please. With you nothing is impossible."

As we came back to our building with the bread, Lisi exclaimed, "Where are those farmers with their wagons?"

"I wonder what happened," I said. "Surely God has answered our prayers."

One of the women came running to us saying, "We do not have to go now. When you left for the bakery, the government officer and the mayor were talking to our women.

Some of the women have small children. They were crying so hard, pleading for mercy, begging them to let us stay here a little longer, until the weather gets warmer. So they decided to let us stay a little while. The mayor told me to tell you that we should divide the bread among us."

"Praise the Lord!" I almost shouted. It was an answer to my prayer, and I am sure my family and others prayed also. The Bible says God "is able to do exceedingly abundantly above all that we ask or think" (Ephesians 3:20). He certainly had done that!

"Those were frightening moments," Mother said, smiling through her tears, "but God answered our prayer."

"I don't know how I can praise God enough," was Ida's thankful reaction.

None of us could. But we tried. We came together for a prayer meeting that evening, and our prayers were praises. God had worked a miracle for us.

V

The Sled

"What do we do now?" Mother asked us children. "God has helped us by stopping the government from transporting us this winter. But in the spring they will surely send us to Siberia. If only Papa were here to help us know what to do!"

Then Mother thought of Uncle Gottlieb. She said, "Children, we have to try to ask our Uncle Gottlieb if he will come and help us out of this town."

"Yes, Mother," I agreed. "But we have to hurry."

Fritz's face lighted up. "It would be so nice if Uncle Gottlieb could come. I love him, and if we are transported, we will never, never see him again."

Our whole family loved Uncle Gottlieb and his family. They were always kind and helpful to us. We felt close to them.

"Lilli," Mother requested, "you go now and send a telegram to Uncle Gottlieb, asking if he would be so kind as to come and help us leave Lichtenburg."

Yes, Mother," I replied, "I will do that right now."

I wired Uncle Gottlieb, "Please come and help us."

Anxiously we waited, praying earnestly that the Lord would speak to Uncle Gottlieb. We knew he did not have a place for us to live, but maybe he would know of a little room for us somewhere. Lichtenburg had no jobs for us. We were too frightened to stay where we were much longer.

Several days later a knock sounded on our door. I opened it and cried out, "Uncle Gottlieb! Uncle! How wonderful to see you!"

He had taken the train to Felsenthal, then walked the 16 kilometers to our hotel room.

"I got your telegram," he announced, "and I have come to help you. I will take you with me. We will find a place for you to live."

This brought great joy to our sad, frightened family. We knew he was sent by God. We had been like sheep without a shepherd, but now the Good Shepherd was giving us someone to show us the way!

Weary from his strenuous journey, Uncle Gottlieb rested for several hours that afternoon. Then he opened his bag and said to Mother, "I brought you a loaf of bread for the trip tomorrow."

"Thank you so much," Mother said. "Now we have food for our trip. I was worried that if you would come to help us, we would not have anything to eat. We still have some money, but there is no food for us to buy."

We all joined in thanking Uncle Gottlieb

for his kindness, tears rolling down our faces.

"I hope some day, Uncle Gottlieb, we can do something nice for you," I said.

"How much luggage do you have?" Uncle Gottlieb asked.

"We do not have very much," I told him. "But how will we get it to the train depot?"

"It is snowing very hard outside," Ida reminded us. "With snow on the streets, a little sled would be just the thing."

Mother approved. "That sounds very good. Then Lilli and Ida can pull the sled."

We all agreed that God had sent the snow for sledding, and that Uncle Gottlieb should make the sled.

Fritz spoke up. "I'd like to help also."

Next day Fritz and Uncle Gottlieb found some old boards outside the hotel and began making a sled.

It was good to have our uncle with us. He looked so much like Papa.

"Have you heard anything from him?" Uncle Gottieb asked Mother.

Mother shook her head sadly. "No. Like thousands of other men, he's never been heard of since he was taken."

"Why did we have war?" Fritz wondered.

We could not answer, though we knew Hitler had wanted to conquer the world.

Mother and Ida got busy packing our few things. I had to go to various government offices to give information about our leaving Lichtenburg. Also I had to contact a doctor.

Travelers by train had to get a certain kind of disinfectant powder from a doctor who then signed certificates for them to show when buying train tickets. The government did not care if we had anything to eat, but it showed great concern about having us disinfected.

By evening the little sled was finished, the packing was done, we were disinfected, and we were ready to leave on the early morning train at five o'clock. This would mean walking the 16 kilometers to the station during the night.

"We should start not later that 2:00 in the morning," we decided. "That will give us around three hours to walk to the depot."

In one way it was hard for us to leave our dear Christian friends in Lichtenburg. We knew we would never see them again since they would be transported to Siberia as soon as the weather turned warmer. How sorry we felt for them! How we wished we could take them all with us!

My family and I had learned to treasure friendship. Going through deep heartaches and crying out together in one accord to the Lord had drawn us Christian refugees together in bonds of love that could not easily be broken.

That evening our friends came to our room for a farewell service. They stayed until we left at 2:00. Our last minutes together were moving ones. We asked each other for forgiveness for any hurts. We sang hymns.

We read the Bible. We shed tears. We put each other in the Lord's hands and prayed, "Lord, keep us faithful until we meet again in our heavenly home where we will never need to say good-by again."

We loaded our luggage onto the sled and fastened it with a rope. Then we stepped out of our little hotel room and said good-by to our dear friends.

Ida and I found sixteen kilometers a long way to pull the sled. In some places there was no snow. Ida was not very strong, and the pulling depended largely on me. It became harder and harder, and we grew more and more weary.

Suddenly, I broke down with exhaustion, unable to take another step. As I slumped onto the sled, I realized I had not taken time for a meal all day. There had been so much to do, along with the excitement of leaving, that I had not thought of eating. Now I saw that even though God supplies our strength, we have to be wise in taking care of our bodies. I had not been very wise, giving my body no food all day and then using it for three hours at night to pull this loaded sled.

I realized I was very hungry. I said, "Mother, could I have a slice of bread?"

That one loaf of bread was all the food we had along. And we could thank Uncle Gottlieb for that.

The slice of bread and a little rest brought new strength to my body. Slowly I felt able to move a little, and Ida and I began to pull the sled again.

We reached the depot to find the train already gone. We had missed it by several minutes. Now we would have to wait many hours for our next connection.

I thought, "And it's all my fault." But there was nothing to do but wait.

In spite of all the kindness Uncle Gottlieb had shown us, we felt some uneasiness about going home with him. We knew he did not have a place for us to live. We knew also he did not have room for us in his tiny house. He himself had lost everything in his escape. He told us he planned to build a house.

"What did he plan to do with us?" we wondered. We did not want to ask. I thought, "If Papa were with us, the two brothers could build together; then we could have our own home again."

Having to bear so much responsibility so young, I missed my father extra much. Perhaps that was one reason I leaned extra hard on my heavenly Father.

In early afternoon we arrived in Eichenthal, the small town where Uncle Gottlieb, Aunt Sophie, and Cousin Angelika lived. Seeing them all again thrilled us. We had to spend some time just looking at each other. Were we really here instead of Siberia? We could not find words to say out loud what we felt in our hearts. With tears rolling down our faces, we said, "Thank you, Uncle Gottlieb, for coming to bring us here. May God bless you for it."

Our first conversation centered around God's wonderful protection. They, like us, had hard months behind them. All of us agreed that we were alive because God had kept His hand of protection over us.

I noticed at once that Uncle and his family lived in one small room. Only one room!

"It used to be a chicken house," Aunt Sophie told us. "Now it is fixed up for a room."

I thought, "How must they feel? They used to be very wealthy. They used to live in a large house. Now they are happy to live in one room."

I glanced around, wondering if there might be another chicken house for us. I saw none.

We had thought Uncle Gottlieb had lost everything when they had to escape. Now they told us how they had saved their money.

"I saw Hitler's defeat coming in the nick of time," Uncle Gottlieb began. "I knew the government would take over the banks, so I did my own banking. See that rag doll? Our daughter and little granddaughter Nelly were living with us while our son-in-law was in the army. We stuffed paper marks into that rag doll and our granddaughter Nelly played with it during our escape. No officers ever questioned rag dolls, so now we have money for building a house."

This uncle, always special to us, seemed extra special now. How nearly he looked like

Papa! What managing ability he had used in his own finances and escape! What kindness he had shown to us in coming for us, in making the sled, in bringing us with him and in saving us from Siberia! We felt like hugging him all the time as we visited in his home.

I had been praying that the Lord would give me a thankful heart in every situation. I had made many vows, promising the Lord I would never stop praising Him for helping us so far, often miraculously. In my desperation I had often prayed like a little child to his parents, using the same words over and over. Always God heard my prayers and kept His promises. That day at my uncle's I realized this even more than ever. I thought about the verse, "Jesus Christ the same yesterday, and today, and for ever" (Hebrews 13:8).

By late afternoon we were sure we could not stay there over night. Fritz spoke up and asked, "Uncle Gottlieb, may I stay with you? I saw your horse in the barn. I love it. If you keep me I can drive your horse. I promise I will do my very best to help you."

Uncle Gottlieb looked at Fritz in compassion and regret. "I am sorry, Fritz, but I cannot keep you now. Sometime later when I have built my own home, then you can come and help me."

"You will be moving in with Aunt Frederika," Uncle Gottlieb then told us. "She lives two miles from here, in Eberfeld."

We knew Aunt Frederika had only a small,

four-room house, including the kitchen. We were told that three of her own children with their families were living with her. They were thirteen; our four would make seventeen.

I said, "Uncle Gottlieb, will there be enough room for us?"

He nodded. "Oh yes. They will make room."

I wondered. I asked myself, "Will Aunt Frederika and all the cousins be friendly to us? Since they did not have to escape, will they feel our heartaches?" My family and I were crushed by the loss of our papa, our home, and everything we could call our own. With our Uncle Gottlieb we could feel at home because he had traveled the same road. He knew from experience what it meant to leave everything behind and flee for his life. But Aunt Frederika had not had the same kind of pain.

About that time I looked out the window and saw a horse-drawn wagon approaching. It was my cousin Robert, a son of Aunt Frederika, coming to take us to their home.

We said good-by to Uncle Gottlieb and his family and thanked them for everything they had done for us. Then we loaded our baggage and ourselves onto the wagon.

While riding with Cousin Robert, we grew more and more excited about meeting Aunt Frederika and the cousins. At the same time we felt more and more uncertain, like sheep without a shepherd. Still, we knew that the

Good Shepherd was leading and keeping us. This gave us new strength and helped us realize it was God's plan for us to move in with Aunt Frederika, even if her family did not know what hardship was. I told myself I would try to be a blessing to them by witnessing. I would tell them how close heaven had seemed when the bullets were dropping around us and how near we had come to going home to be with Jesus.

Thinking thus, I felt like saying with the psalmist: "I will praise thee, O Lord my God, with all my heart: and I will glorify thy name for evermore" (Psalm 86:12).

VI

AUNT FREDERIKA

When the wagon stopped in front of Aunt Frederika's house, my heartbeat quickened and I drew a deep, anxious breath. Would this big family really want to take us in?

Aunt Frederika and some of the cousins came out to greet us. Then they took us to the second floor and showed us the room where we were to live. We would share it at night with Cousins Elvira and Helga and Elvira's small son who slept in a baby bed.

Twin beds awaited Mother and Fritz. They had just been nailed together, unvarnished and filled with fresh, clean straw. Ida and I would sleep in another bed. That large room with all those beds looked like a hospital room to us. We were grateful for it, though, even for the straw mattresses. Sleeping on straw in a bed would be much better than sleeping on a pile of straw on a floor.

Soon the relatives all went to their rooms, leaving us alone to get settled. As Mother stood beside those twin beds, she sighed. I knew she was thinking, "It was war, not our management, that made us poor. Must we still be treated like refugees here? I am sure my sister-in-law has a well-furnished house, with mattresses and sheets on all the other beds. On ours she has straw and no sheets."

Knowing mother's thoughts, I looked at her and said, "Mother, be of good cheer. What are we in this world? Not more than just little grains of dust. Jesus, the Son of God, came to this world. He is the King of kings. Yet there was no room for Him either. He was born in a stable and put in a manger filled with straw."

"Yes, Lilli," Mother answered. "That is true. I am very sorry. I don't want to complain. I too promised the Lord that I would always be thankful, but sometimes I can't help feeling hurt."

A little table and four chairs stood at the end of the twin beds. We four gathered around that table, and Mother took out the precious Bible which we had found on the street during our escape.

She read Isaiah 26:3, 4. We looked at each other through tears, and joined in prayer. The burden of our prayer was, "Lord, help us to trust in Thee every minute of our lives, in every situation. Give us the perfect peace that comes from having our minds stayed on Thee."

After prayer we began to share with each other times when God had given us peace in the past during frightening moments.

Mother began. "I will never forget the night the soldiers told us we would be killed before the night was over. I certainly felt heavenly peace flooding my soul that night."

"Yes, Mother," Ida added, "I was so happy I knew how to pray."

"It is wonderful," I testified, "to be ready for heaven in a moment like that. I could sense there were angels around us."

"No one knows how I felt," Ida said, "when the other farm girls left for their homes and I was standing there all alone, wondering whether my family escaped without me. I am so thankful I can be with my family. Thousands of other young people were separated from their parents. I know the Lord is my Shepherd. Mother, would you please read Psalm 23?"

"Yes, Ida," mother answered happily.

Mother paused as she came to verse four. "Yea, though I walk through the valley of the shadow of death, I will fear no evil: for thou art with me; thy rod and thy staff they comfort me."

"Children!" Mother exclaimed. "The Bible is so true. We did walk through the valley of the shadow of death, and God did take the fear away, and He filled our frightened hearts with peace. Praise His holy name forever!"

"The Lord has also been good to me," Fritz put in. "I love the Lord since I accepted Him as my personal Saviour, and I so enjoyed praying with those boys in Lichtenburg."

As we continued to share, Ida paused, "It seems to me I can hear voices behind that wall. There must be more people living in this house."

"I think so too," Mother added. "We have not met all our relatives yet."

Just then a door opened slowly from the far side of our room, and four people called out, "Good evening."

"Good evening," we answered.

"Robert has not come in yet, but we wanted to meet you. My name is Mrs. Lick," said the oldest one. "These are my grandchildren, Rita and Sigfried. This is my daughter Anchen, the wife of Robert who went with the horse and wagon to bring you here. First of all, we want to welcome you to our large family. We do not want to interrupt you, but we heard you talking, and we wanted to get acquainted."

"Oh, that is fine, Mrs. Lick," I told her. "We were sharing the wonderful things of the Lord and how He has brought us this far."

"Oh, do you love the Lord?" Anchen asked.

"We surely do," I declared.

"So does my family," answered Mrs. Lick. "We also had to escape and leave everything behind. We are thankful to be alive."

Knowing this about them helped us get acquainted fast. I told them, "We are so happy to meet you as our relatives, and also happy to know you love Jesus. Can we all join hands and pray, thanking the Lord for bringing us together?"

Mrs. Lick's face lighted. She stretched her hands toward us and said, "Yes, let's pray."

We all joined hands and hearts, and with one accord we thanked God for keeping us alive through the many dangers.

As we finished praying, we heard a knock on our door. Aunt Frederika was there, inviting us to come down for supper.

The milk soup and rye bread tasted very good. We had not even seen milk for a long time.

While sitting around that large table after supper and visiting with each other, I could not help thinking about those two beds with straw in them.

"How am I going to cover them?" I asked myself. "We lost all our bed sheets." I was too timid to ask my aunt if she would lend us some sheets until we could buy some.

After supper we went back to our room to unpack our things.

"Thank God!" I suddenly cried out, holding up and unfolding a large piece of old used material I had found in the woods in Lichtenburg. "This will cover the straw."

As we finished fixing up our room the best we could, I glanced at Mother. I saw tears in her eyes.

"Mother, what is wrong?" I asked.

"Children," she poured out, "If Papa would just be with us. . . ." The grief of his absence was always with her.

"That is true," I agreed, "but think of all we have to be thankful for. The rest of the family is still together, and our Aunt Frederika was kind enough to take us in."

"We will work hard," Ida added consolingly," and someday, the Lord willing, we will have our own home again. In spite of straw beds and loneliness, we still have a roof over our heads."

The next morning Aunt Frederika showed us a wood stove in the hall on the first floor which we would share with Cousin Robert's family for cooking. But what would we cook? She made no offer or suggestion.

Aunt Frederika had a large farm. Her husband was dead and her two sons were still missing from the war, so most of the farm work had to be done by us girls.

Life grew hard for us with Aunt Frederika. Day after day Ida and I had to work in the field. Fritz went to school. Mother helped with housework and with feeding the animals. Most of the time we did not have enough to eat. We had ration cards from the government, but there was little food in the stores. Since the government did not pay farmers much for their produce, Aunt Frederika in turn did not pay us for our work. Still, her table was well set. She butchered pigs for meat. She had milk and eggs from her cows and chickens. Sometimes she gave us a little milk, occasionally a few eggs, and once in a great while a bit of butter.

We had promised God to be thankful in every situation. Now we tried hard to thank Him in this one. We gave special thanks the times Uncle Gottlieb and Aunt Sophie would bring us flour for baking bread. We always felt special thanks on Cousin Selma's bread baking days also. Cousin Selma, a war widow, lived close to her mother, Aunt Frederika, but not in the same house. With no oven of her own, she always came to her mother's home to bake her bread. And nearly always she left a freshly-baked loaf with us. Dear, big-hearted, unselfish Selma! In spite of the griefs war had brought her, she loved to help lighten the load for other sufferers.

In spite of the loneliness and lack of food, we trusted our heavenly Father to give us endurance and make a way out for us. I told my family, "Let's take good courage. We know this will not be for very long. We have relatives in Canada and in the U.S.A. Perhaps the Lord will lead us to them."

How different it was for those who did not know the Lord and who did not know how to pray. Many gave way to discouragement and despair. Some even killed their children to spare them from the hopelessness ahead.

My cousin Inge witnessed such a tragedy. On arising one morning and looking out her window, she saw three people lying in her neighbor's field.

"What is going on in Schmuland's field?" she wondered, hurrying out to see whether they needed help.

They were all dead. Early that morning Mrs. Schmuland, the mother in that home, had taken her 26-year-old sister, her 20-year-old daughter, and her 18-year-old son out into the field. There, evidently by their own consent, she had cut their throats with a knife. Then, when attempting to cut her own throat, she regained her sanity. She ran into the house to her husband, put her arms around him, and asked him if he could forgive her for what she had just done. A soldier, staying in their house, learned about her outrageous action and shot her there in front of her husband. Though Mr. Schmuland had one son in the army (who later returned), he did not know how to cope with the shock and grief of his great loss.

Many times afterward I saw Mr. Schmuland in the cemetery beside the graves of his loved ones. There were two white rocks among the tombs. On one he would place his hat. On the other he would sit and mourn. People could not find words to comfort him. When they tried, he would say, "My family would be with me today if we had not had the war. My wife was a good woman. I know she dearly loved her family. Fear caused it all—fear of the future."

Before the war Mr. Schmuland had been a very wealthy farmer, owning thousands of acres of land and many houses. War had stripped the family of all these. Now, he had nothing but memories and bitterness.

One Sunday morning as Ida and I were walking to church, two other women joined us. One of them began telling us how nearly she had once come to such tragic action. She said, "I planned to kill my 15-year-old son."

I looked at her and exclaimed, "You really wanted to kill your own son?"

"Yes. We were so frightened about what would happen to us. I thought it would be better for him to be dead." Then she added, "But somehow I couldn't do it."

Ida asked her, "Aren't you glad today that you still have your son?"

"Oh, I thank God every day that my son is still with me. I could never have forgiven myself if I had killed him. He is my only child. I love him dearly. But that is what fear did to me."

"What terrible things war can do to people!" I thought.

One quiet Saturday evening after our work was done and we were sitting in our room, we heard a knock. I hurried to open the door.

"Oh, what a surprise!" I exclaimed. "Uncle Gottlieb and Aunt Sofie have come to see us."

We had much to talk about. During our conversation Uncle Gottlieb asked, "How do you like it here?"

Mother answered, "We are grateful to have a roof over our heads, but—if we only would have enough to eat."

Aunt Sofie said sympathetically, "Don't worry. We will help you. We will give you some flour, and you can bake some bread."

Their kindness touched us deeply. Though

they had lost much through the war, they were willing to help us.

"Can I come with you now?" Fritz asked them as they arose to leave.

"Our home is not finished yet," Aunt Sofie reminded him. "We will see when you can come. Next week we will bring the flour we promised you."

"Thank you so much for everything, Uncle Gottlieb and Aunt Sofie," we said while wiping our tears. "We will remember you the rest of our lives."

That visit on such a lonely evening was a great blessing to us. It gave us new hope. Also it brought us some bread. Our aunt and uncle had ministered to us in the method Jesus blessed when He said, "Inasmuch as ye have done it unto one of the least of these my brethren, ye have done it unto me" (Matthew 25:40).

Spring came to little Eberfeld. Leaf buds swelled on the trees. Flowers began to open.

Along with the beautiful weather, came new friends. Elizabeth, the first of these, really came to visit my cousins Robert and Anchen. I felt Christian warmth in her the moment I met her, and soon she and I were singing hymns and praying together. I confided in her what Jesus meant to me, how disappointed I felt about the spiritual coldness in the church I was attending, and how I would enjoy getting to a good church service. I told her our father had been a minister who preached Scripturally sound sermons, and asked her where we could find a church that would meet our need.

"I know one, Lilli," Elizabeth assured me. "In the town where I live."

"Oh, really?" I asked. "But how would I get there? Do you live very far from here?"

"Only an hour by train. Come to visit me some Saturday, and on Sunday we can go to church together. I am sure you would get a blessing there."

"May I come this next Saturday?" I asked her excitedly.

"I would love to have you," she answered.

Before leaving, Elizabeth gave me her address, directions for finding her, and an *auf wiedersehen* that lengthened into "I will see you again next Saturday."

I answered happily, "Yes, the Lord willing, I will be there."

"This will really be something," I told myself. "Leaving this farm for a weekend, getting away from the hard work, fellowshipping with Elizabeth, meeting other Christians, and listening to a sound, Spirit-filled sermon!"

I did have things to be thankful for here with Aunt Frederika, of course. Five in her household were Christians. Cousin Robert was an ordained minister. Sometimes on Sundays we had Bible reading and prayer together. This was helpful, but my soul was not fully satisfied.

Since food was a real problem in those days, guests often needed to take food supplies with them. In my case Cousin Irma gave me a small bag of potatoes to take along for my weekend at Elizabeth's.

I put the potatoes into a backpack, so my hands would be free for my clothesbag and purse. After joyous good-bys to family and relatives, I walked the three miles to the Eberfeld depot and boarded the train.

I found Elizabeth's home without difficulty and rang the doorbell.

"How nice to see you!" Elizabeth welcomed. "I was wondering if you would find me. Sit down and make yourself at home. I will make some tea."

Elizabeth put chairs beside a little round coffee table, and as we sipped tea together, we shared the wonderful things the Lord had done for us.

Suddenly Elizabeth looked right at me and asked, "Lilli, what do you mean by 'a good church'? I told you we had a good church here in my town. I meant we have one that I consider good."

"What do I mean by a good church? I mean—when the minister speaks in all boldness that Jesus Christ is the only way to heaven and that He alone can forgive our sins and fill our hearts with joy and peace."

Elizabeth nodded, "I thought that was what you meant. We have that kind here."

The next morning. I found the people at

church friendly. They made me feel right at home. The minister preached a good, sound sermon—the first of its kind I had heard since the beginning of the tragedy and fear in the country. It blessed my heart and filled me with new strength.

After the service I met Anita, a Christian girl and a member of that church. She invited me to her home. I said good-by to Elizabeth, thanked her for the nice time she had shown me, and went with Anita.

Anita lived with her sister Gretchen and their father. After dinner we began to share some of the recent tragedies of our lives.

"Two of my brothers were killed in the war," Anita began. "We lost our beautiful home. All this is sad, but things could have been worse if Hitler had won the war. He was against a Bible-believing church. If he had won, Christians who really love the Lord would be suffering persecution now."

"I believe that, Anita. My sister and I had Bible names. We were ordered to change them."

Gretchen, who had been listening, looked at me in great surprise and said, "Oh, really? I hadn't heard about such a law. Different parts of Germany must have had different laws."

Gretchen wanted to know more. "What were your Bible names, and where are they found in the Bible?"

I told her, "My name was Leah, and Ida's was Rachel. They are found in Genesis 29:16.

"And Laban had two daughters: the name of the elder was Leah, and the name of the younger was Rachel."

"How did you feel about changing your name?" Anita asked.

"We could not say anything; we had to obey the law," I said.

I had a wonderful time of sharing with these dear Christians. But time passed by too quickly. I had to get back to my family and to the farm.

Before I left these new friends, we prayed together. All of us praised God for keeping us safe through hardships and dangers, for putting songs of thanks in our hearts, and for making us living proofs that the Bible is true. We all knew what God meant when He said to Joshua, "I will be with thee: I will not fail thee, nor forsake thee" (Joshua 1:5).

Back home I reported happily to my family that I had found a spiritual church and had enjoyed blessed fellowship with my new Christian friends.

Ida said, "I'd like to be in a spiritual church too. When you go again, may I go along?"

"Surely," I said. And after that we went together.

Our family had now been at Aunt Frederika's a whole year. We longed and prayed for a better life. What good were we doing here? What future did we have? When could we find work that would bring in earnings and allow us to have a home of our own again?

We knew we had grandparents and an uncle and aunt in Canada. We knew some of Mother's cousins lived somewhere in the United States, but we had lost all their addresses during our escape and wanderings. We often said to each other, "How wonderful it would be to receive mail from them again!"

On the next visit to Elizabeth's church, I met a very friendly woman named Mrs. Bauman. She began telling me about her relatives in Canada. Excitedly I asked her, "Do you receive mail from them?"

"Oh, yes," she answered with a big smile.

Feeling sure that God had brought about this meeting with Mrs. Bauman, I asked my new friend, "If I would write down all our names, birthdates, and addresses, would you be so kind as to send them to your relatives in Canada? Perhaps there would be a way to advertise them so that our relatives would know to write to us."

"I will gladly do that for you," Mrs. Bauman offered. "And I am sure my relatives in Canada would be more than happy to have your names put in some kind of church paper."

Overjoyed, I wrote our names, birthdates, and Aunt Frederika's address and handed my list to her.

New hope came to my family and me. In a dream I saw mail coming from Canada and from the United States. Would this become another miracle for us? How thankful I was for

Elizabeth who invited me to her church! I was certain God was answering our prayers.

"Will there really be a better future for us?" Mother wondered.

I put all possible encouragement into my answering words, "Yes, Mother, I do hope so."

Ideas began crowding into my mind.

I had a girl friend, Erika, living in West Germany. We wrote to each other regularly.

"Why don't I write to Erika?" I asked myself and my family. "Maybe she could give us suggestions."

Through Erika I made contact with a mission in West Germany which helped people get visas for immigrating to America. They sent us forms to fill out. When we returned them, we were informed that we could never immigrate to America from East Germany.

"Somehow we must get into West Germany," we decided.

"If our relatives in America should write us, and we are no longer here in East Germany," Mother thought out loud, "I am sure Aunt Frederika would forward the letters to us."

Yet we were reluctant to leave. Ida expressed our apprehension, "It is frightening to step out again, not knowing what could happen to us."

I looked at Fritz, just fourteen years old. I looked at Ida, now nineteen. I looked at Mother, forty-nine. Should we go? I was used to taking charge. But in this case, did I want to face the responsibility of four lives?

I tried to weigh our past, present, and future fairly as I put my thinking into words. "We all have hope for a better life if we get to West Germany. We have no future if we stay here. But how can we cross the border without permission? If we are caught, what might happen to us? Would there be hard punishment?"

"If we could find a person who has crossed the border before," Mother suggested, "he could advise us if it is very dangerous. We will pray that God will send us the right person.

We all agreed to pray.

Two weeks went by. Nothing happened. Then one day as we were all together in Aunt Frederika's kitchen, we heard a knock.

We opened the door and welcomed in a stranger named Alexander. He had traveled by train many hours, then walked the three miles to our town, trying to buy some food for his family.

During our conversation with him, we told him we were planning to cross the border but didn't know the way and were rather frightened.

"Oh," Mr. Alexander began assuring us, "it is not hard to cross over into West Germany. I have been to West Germany a number of times. I have seen people crossing by the hundreds every day."

"Oh, is that true?" I asked. "But how?"

"I am going to West Germany again," he

told us. "I would be very happy to show you the way."

"Oh, really?" I answered with eagerness. "This would be wonderful. When are you going?"

"I cannot tell you the exact day, but I will come to meet you here. Then we can go together."

This sounded very good to us.

Mr. Alexander turned to Mother and offered his terms. "I promise that I will come back and help you over the border if you give me in advance a little something for my family to eat."

We looked at each other. Could we trust this stranger? Would he really come back to help us? Would he lead us the right way? It would be wonderful to have a good leader who knows the way, we thought, while we inwardly prayed.

On the other hand, did we have any food to give away? After questioning among ourselves, Mother reminded us, "Our neighbor, Mr. Schmidt, gave us a bag of potatoes."

"And yesterday," I added, "I bought our ration butter for this month, one-quarter of a pound."

Hearing us, Mr. Alexander said, "If you give me that, I would be very happy." He assured us he was telling the truth and would be back for us.

"Let's give him that butter and the bag of potatoes," Mother decided. "That is all we have."

"Is this the answer to our prayer?" we wondered as we watched him leave. "Will he really come back, or is he a crook?" He had given us no date for returning, and no address."

"He will have a couple of good meals from us," Ida thought out loud. "We should have asked him if he believes in God."

"If it's true that hundreds of people are crossing the border every day," Fritz reasoned, "it must not be so hard."

Feeling more encouraged and less frightened now, we waited for Alexander to return. One week went by. Two weeks went by. Should we wait any longer? Would he ever return? Not knowing his address, we could not write to him. Had we put our faith in an undependable man? In our desperation had we trusted unwisely?

"I was sure he was honest," Mother said.

After much praying, waiting, and wondering, we gradually gave up looking for Mr. Alexander. Mother had another idea and said, "If we could meet other people who are planning to cross the border, we could go with them."

One day on my way to the bakery for our ration bread, I met an elderly couple, Mr. and Mrs. Helbert. During our conversation Mrs. Helbert informed me with a big smile, "Tomorrow morning we are planning to take the train to cross the border into West Germany."

All excited, I asked, "Do you know the way."

"No, but we will find some people who know the way."

She sounded so confident, as though there was no danger ahead.

"We are four in our family," I informed her. "May we go with you?"

Mr. Helbert readily told me the time when they would be at the train depot to leave.

I hurried home with my bread and my exciting story. "I met a friendly couple at the bakery," I bubbled. "They are ready to take the train tomorrow to cross the border into West Germany. Are we still going to wait for Mr. Alexander?"

Fritz shrugged. "He'll probably never come back to help us."

Mother said sadly, "It is too bad. I believed that man and gave him our last food. But what can we do now?"

After discussing our situation at length, we decided we should try to get ready to go with the Helberts the next day. I said, "We've prayed much about it for weeks, and if it is God's will for us to go tomorrow, then everything will fall into place for us."

Before we could leave, however, we had to have identification papers from our town government office. Anyone changing location in Germany had to have such papers.

I took courage and went to our Eberfeld office. On the way I prayed for help from God for an answer to give if I would be asked why I needed such papers. The papers were handed to me without any questions, and my thankfulness to God knew no limits. "I can do all things through Christ which strengtheneth me" (Philippians 4:13) fit me personally just then. The Lord had helped me take the first legal step toward our goal. He would help with all the other steps, I told myself.

My family gathered around me on my return home, asking if I had the papers.

"Yes, I have them, and here it is in writing that we are leaving tomorrow, Wednesday, July 16, 1947. I learned that here in Eberfeld officers don't try to keep people from going. They leave that to the police at the border.

Our relatives in Aunt Frederika's house asked, "Are you really leaving?"

"Yes, we are going to try," we told them. "We might be back if it is impossible to cross the border."

"It is late afternoon already," Mother reminded us. "We have to hurry to get ready if we are leaving tomorrow."

I will never forget that Tuesday afternoon with all its last-minute pressures.

Mr. Schmidt, our neighbor, came over while we were packing our few things. He asked, "What are you doing? Why are you all so excited?"

We told him our plans.

"Oh, no, you can't leave tomorrow," he informed us, now very excited himself.

"Why not?" I questioned. "I have the identification papers. Is there something else that can hold us back? Please, Mr. Schmidt, tell us. Why can't we leave?"

He explained. "I just came from the town office. They told me you have a lot of money coming from the government, but only the papers have arrived. The money itself has not come in yet."

Had we heard correctly? Would the government give us money?

"Yes," Mr. Schmidt repeated, "to all who have lost everything the government will give money to help them get started again."

"What can I possibly do now?" I asked. "The identification papers say we are leaving tomorrow. They all know this in the office. Will they still give me the money?"

"Lilli," Mother decided, "you have to go and try. Maybe they will give it to you."

I prayed, "God, please give me enough strength to go back."

Fearful and embarrassed, I mounted my cousin's bicycle and went. I entered the office almost unable to speak. Haltingly, I asked pardon for returning a second time, just an hour after the first time, and tried very politely to repeat what Mr. Schmidt had just told us. Inwardly I kept praying, "Jesus, you are so wonderful to me. Please help me to say the right words and to make the right decisions."

"It would be so nice," I said aloud to the

officers behind the desk, "if we could receive that money. We do need it desperately."

They listened to me, considered in friendly silence for awhile, then told me we would receive 1,000 German marks. To get it, though, I would have to sign a receipt that stated I had already received the money. Then we could use that receipt to borrow money from our relatives who in turn would be paid back by the government when the money came in.

The decision was a big one for me to make, but with shaking hands I signed that receipt.

Terrifying thoughts went though my mind as I left that office. Had I made the right decision? What a lot of money to borrow when we were leaving the country! Could I believe the government? Would they actually give it back to our relatives after we were gone?

Again I yet remembered that God had never failed me. I believed He would provide this time also.

On my way home new fears gripped me, making me almost unable to ride the bicycle. What would Mother say? What would my relatives say? Would any of them be willing to lend us that amount of money? They might be afraid of losing it.

My family and relatives surrounded me as I entered the house, wondering what results I had. With stuttering voice I told them, "We will receive 1,000 German marks. They asked me to sign the statement. I did not know what to do, but I signed it. They advised me to borrow the money from relatives, and assured me when the money comes in, there would be no problem. Whoever lends it to us can go to the office then and pick it up."

There I stood, surrounded by relatives, wondering which one I should ask first. Then I turned to Aunt Frederika and asked, "Would you be so kind as to lend us that amount of money?"

She gave me a strange look and said, "I don't have that much."

I felt hurt over this unexpected answer. I knew Aunt Frederika had the money, and it seemed she should have been the one to help us. We had worked for her a year without pay, and without sufficient food. Didn't she, of all people, owe it to us?

I continued to pray inwardly. I had signed the statement. What should I do?

I did not need to decide. God did that. He sent Cousin Selma, a war widow, to us. Selma had come in to say good-by. As I tried to collect myself after the let-down from Aunt Frederika, Cousin Selma turned to me and volunteered, "I will lend you the money. I have lost so much in my life that if I should lose a little more it would not make any difference to me."

Her love and generosity amazed me. I thanked her from the depth of my heart and wept for joy.

Now I could understand why Mr. Alexander had not come. If he had come and we had gone with him, we would have missed the money from the government. Again God had planned for us and had taken care of us. In amazement I joined the psalmist, David, and exclaimed, "What is man, that thou art mindful of him? and the son of man, that thou visitest him?" (Psalm 8:4).

Our family spent some happy moments rehearsing the miraculous way God was working for us.

"But, children," Mother said, "we must go to our Uncle Gottlieb to say good-by."

Of course! Dear, good Uncle Gottlieb, and Aunt Sofie—the ones who always helped us in our greatest neeeds! We must go there at once.

When we told Aunt Frederika, she said, "It is only four miles to walk by the road, but through the fields it is a lot closer."

"But it is getting dark outside," Robert cautioned.

We hurriedly finished our packing and started for Uncle Gottlieb's. We walked as fast as we could, but darkness overtook us in the woods. We became frightened and held fast to each other.

"What will happen to us if we get lost in this woods?" Fritz asked. "I once read a story about Hansel and Gretchen. They got lost in a woods and finally arrived in a little house where an old witch lived."

"I am sure we will find our way through this

woods, Fritz," Mother comforted.

We surprised Uncle Gottlieb with our plans to catch the train next morning for crossing the border. He had no objections, though, and said, "May the Lord be with you and protect you."

We visited a short time and thanked Uncle Gottlieb and Aunt Sofie for every kindness they had shown us.

On our way home that night, we had little to say. Many of our thoughts were too deep for words. How could any of us tell the rest his feelings about leaving Aunt Frederika? How could we express the gratitude we owed her for at least taking us in and for serving as a bridge in our destiny? How could we tell each other the thanks we felt for the miracle God was working in our behalf?

How strange our room looked to us as we entered it for the last time and made our way around among our baggaged things! Once more we counted the packs. They totaled twelve. That meant three pieces for each of us—one piece on our back and one in each hand. Mother would carry the three lightest ones, I would take the bulkiest, Fritz and Ida would handle the in-between ones.

Mother looked at her three pieces and wondered aloud, "Will we have to walk very far? Will we find our way across the border?"

All of us wondered those same things, but

we knew we should not let our minds dwell on them. We prayed together, turned out the light, and made our way to our beds, calling out our last goodnights in this house.

VII

FIVE-GALLON GAS CANS

Daylight on Wednesday morning found us leaving our room, after a hot breakfast, for our journey toward the border. Some of the relatives in the house helped us get our luggage downstairs and make our final preparations for departure.

In the rush and commotion, I slipped quietly from our room to the attic for a few quiet moments alone. There I poured out my fears to my heavenly Father. There I thanked Him for His past help in every need. There I promised Him my trust. There I besought Him for guidance and safety through the risks and uncertainties ahead.

As our relatives gathered around us in the driveway, we prayed, putting ourselves into the hands of God. Then we sang that old, familiar German hymn.
(written by Julie von Hausmann, in 1867)

"Lord, take my hand and lead me
    unto the end;
In life and death I need Thee, O
    blessed Friend;
I cannot live without Thee for one

brief day;
Lord, be Thou ever near me, and
lead the way."

It was a blessed moment which I will never forget.

As we said good-by with many tears, we knew if we crossed the border, we might never meet again on earth.

Cousin Robert, who had brought us by wagon from Uncle Gottlieb's to Aunt Frederika's, now had the horse and wagon ready to take us to the train depot.

We loaded our baggage onto the wagon, seated ourselves beside Robert, called our final farewells, and left.

While riding to the depot, I kept wondering whether the Helberts would be there. But to my relief, they were there, waiting for us.

We bought train tickets to the station nearest the border, said good-by to Robert, thanked him for bringing us, and wished him the Lord's blessing in his ministry. Then we took a last look at the station and the familiar surroundings, boarded the train, and were off.

Now we found ourselves on a rolling train with the Helberts. Many things had happened in a matter of hours. I could hardly believe our departure was true and not just a dream. Inwardly I prayed, "Oh God, please be with us."

We traveled silently, keeping our jumbled

thoughts to ourselves.

Arriving at our destination that afternoon, we stepped off the train, looked around somewhat bewildered, and made our way into the depot.

Now what? we all wondered. Where do we go? What do we do? What do we say? Dare we ask anyone for any kind of help or direction? Which way is the border?

Mother drew a deep breath and admitted, "I am glad I did not know it would be so frightening. I thought we would step out of the train and see other people crossing the border. I thought we would join them and walk across without any problem."

"Yes, Mother," Ida agreed, "this is another new experience."

I added, "But I believe the Lord will bring some people to help us. Let's pray for a miracle."

While the family stayed with the baggage, I tried to find a place to be alone with God. I saw a woods outside the depot and a path leading into it. During the time we waited, I don't know how many times I went there to pray, overwhelmed by what I saw and heard around me and by the fearfulness of the way ahead.

We saw German soldiers returning from Russian prison camps, hardly able to walk. They looked wasted almost to skin and bone. We were told thousands of prisoners were dying of starvation on their way home. I thought, "Oh, God, all these innocent people that have to suffer! They didn't want a war."

On my trips to the woods, I prayed for these sufferers and for our own family in our dire need. We were not hungry or thirsty. Tragedy around us took hunger and thirst from us. We were fearful and helpless, however, about our future. I begged the Lord as a child does his parents. "Lord, please help us, please, Lord, one more time. We have no other help but Thee, Lord. I promise I will always praise Thee."

Our family had prayed so much about leaving Aunt Frederika's and we had felt it was the Lord's will we should try to cross the border. Had we made a mistake? None of us knew the way. Should we have waited for Mr. Alexander? He had told us he knew how to cross over.

Such thoughts went through my mind, and I prayed, "Lord, if we have made a mistake, please forgive us. Please take us by Your hand. Your Word says, 'The Lord is on my side; I will not fear: what can man do unto me?' (Psalm 118:6). I know these promises are true. Please take all my fear away. When you are with us, man cannot do any harm to us."

We met two boys, Hans and Peter, in the depot. They told us they had just come from the West. We asked them if they would help us over the border to West Germany. We offered to pay them, but they refused.

Peter turned to me and said, "If you did not know the way to cross the border, you should have stayed home."

"Yes, Peter," I replied, embarrassed. "That is true. But a man named Alexander came to us a couple of weeks ago and told us it is not so hard to cross over. Mr. Alexander promised to help us. We believed him. He asked us for food. We gave him the last food we had, hoping he would help us, but he never showed up. Please, Peter," I begged, "help us."

I could not see any sign of mercy on his part.

We did much praying that evening and night there in the depot. God talked to those boys, and at 9:00 the next morning they came to us saying, "We are willing to help you over the border."

"How wonderful!" Mother said. "This makes us very happy."

"What shall I carry?" Hans asked.

"Here, take this," I answered.

Peter offered also. "I am strong. You can give me the heaviest piece."

Mother told him, "You can carry this one; this is heavy."

How happy we were for the help these boys gave us! Without them we could not have walked very far with so much to carry.

Mr. and Mrs. Helbert were still with us but they did not have much luggage to carry.

We started walking, thankful that God had

given us a beautiful, sunshiny day.

In our hearts, happiness and fear struggled with each other. We felt happy to be on our way and to have help and guidance. But we were fearful that everyone who saw us with all the stuff we were carrying would know we were trying to cross the border.

Our fears mounted when, by mistake, Peter and Hans led us directly in front of the police station. They had tried to take a shortcut and had lost their way. Frightened, we tried to hide behind a little shack on one side of the street.

On that same street policemen on motorcycles raced back and forth patroling the border. We could not run away. We prayed and cried, shaking with fear and asking ourselves, "Why did the boys bring us here if they knew another way?"

I remember noticing the time, 10:00 a.m., when the police came to us. They had been watching us from the high tower. They had seen us trying to hide. They knew exactly how many we were, and even what clothes we were wearing. They took us to a large prison room and locked us in behind iron bars.

Our family had never been in prison before, and it gave us an embarrassing and terrible feeling to be there now. We all had to stand or sit on the floor, as there was not even one chair.

Ida groaned, "How long will they keep us here? And what will happen next?"

Fritz asked, "Are we doing something so bad that we have to be in prison?"

"Yes, Fritz" I told him. "At least they think so. We are trying to cross the border without permission."

"Why didn't you get a permission?" Fritz asked again.

"Because the East German government doesn't want people to leave the country."

"I never thought it would be so difficult to cross the border," said Mrs. Helbert.

We all became very quiet, thinking much but saying little. Some of us were praying. Now and then the police brought in more people who had tried to cross the border. By morning the room was packed.

At 7:00 that morning we were all called out and lined up. One policeman was assigned to every nine people. They meant to make sure no one would run away.

Suspecting they would walk us somewhere, Mother said, "What will I do if we have to walk for many hours? Will I be able to take it? Will they let us rest a little? Will we get very thirsty? This is going to be a hot July day. There are no coffee shops anywhere. If I get sick, there probably will be no doctor available."

"Mother," I said, "I am very sure the Lord will give you the strength you need."

We had to walk until 3:00 in the afternoon. Much of this time I was silently praying for strength to endure the hard journey. Thankfully, we found that the police (German) were kind, but they had to do their duty. Every several hours they would call out, "Rest!" Then we all put our luggage down and sat on it.

Mother still had some cake she had baked before we left Aunt Frederika. On one such rest, she opened the bag and gave each of us a piece of that cake. We had nothing to drink. But we could rest for only several minutes until the police called out, "Start walking again!" We took our luggage on our backs or in our hands and resumed walking. We felt like prisoners of war.

I noticed people watching us. Some smiled, though we did not know whether their smiles meant sympathy with us or with the police. We had no chance to speak to anybody.

Our family was amazed at the way the Lord provided our necessary strength. Concerned about Mother, I frequently asked her, "Mother, are you okay?" Always she would reply, "Yes, I am still able to walk."

At 3:00 that afternoon, we arrived at another prison and were locked in again, women in one room and men in another.

Most of us women had something along to eat. In the door between us and the men we noticed a hole cut out with a pocket knife. Knowing that Fritz and the two boys we had hired were in that other room, we cut our cake in strips and pushed it through the hole for them to eat. So did Mrs. Helbert for her husband, and other women for their men.

After hours of waiting, we were called to a government office. The officer asked us, "Why are you trying to cross the border?"

We told him we were going to visit our friends, too much afraid to tell him the whole truth. We would visit Erika in West Germany, but we wanted to go on to America.

"No, no" the officer told us. "You cannot go to West Germany. Close by is the train depot. There you can buy your tickets to go back where you came from."

Our family, Peter and Hans, and the Helberts walked to that train depot. Very discouraged, we sat in the waiting room, not knowing what to do.

"What will you do?" I asked the Helberts.

"We are going back to our home, where we came from," they answered. "You are younger. You can take more hardships. We are too old to struggle any more."

"Should we really buy tickets for the trip back to Aunt Frederika?" Mother asked.

Ida shook her head. "She does not have enough room for us in her small house."

We prayed, "Jesus, please help us. Is there no other way than going back? We have spent many hours in prison and have walked eight hours. Almost all our strength is gone."

A great storm arose in my heart, and with tears I began to search my heart. I cried, "Oh, Lord, show me where I have failed. Please

107

forgive me, Father. Please listen to my cry."

I felt like the disciples in the ship when they said, "Master, carest thou not that we perish?" (Mark 4:38). I reminded the Lord, "We have seen many miracles. You spared us from being sent to Siberia. You even provided money for us before we left Aunt Frederika. Lord, please show us the way now. I promise I will always praise Thee."

As we sat there in the depot, Peter came rushing in. "A passenger train is all checked and ready to pull out for West Germany. Let's run and jump on that train. Hans, help take the luggage. Please hurry, hurry!"

We said good-by to Mr. and Mrs. Helbert. They went their way, and we tried again to cross over.

To me this seemed wrong. I held back. But the boys grabbed our luggage. My family and I had to follow.

We barely got on the train when it started, then suddenly stopped. Something was wrong. I grew very frightened. In the first place, I thought it was wrong to get on that train, and now I knew we would be caught. Police were already calling, "Everyone show your British Identification Cards."

We had no British Identification Cards. What could we do? Shaking with fear, we tried to pray, but we felt almost too guilty to pray.

When the officer reached us and found we had no cards he became very angry. He grabbed part of our luggage and threw it out the door. He told us we would be put in prison for ten days, after which time he would make sure we would take the train back to where we came from.

He then took us back to the same prison from which we had come one hour before, and left us there with another guard.

This other guard checked our papers and told us if we would clean the prison, he would release us.

Peter, Hans, Fritz, Ida, and I cleaned as fast as we could. Mother rested first. She was worn out from fear and walking and heavy carrying.

When we had the cleaning done, the guard kept his promise and let us go, warning us to take the other direction so as not to be seen by the officer who had brought us there.

By now it was sundown. We started out in the direction our guard told us, but didn't know where to go from there. Someone told us to ask the advice of certain workers in the hay fields. We walked on boards and rocks through the swampy land and across the ditches. Finally we came to the hay field. Here a man directed us past a certain house and along a path that would lead us to bushes along the river which formed the border.

We made our way to the bushes and hid where we could hear and see without being seen. Behind us motorcycles roared, and we knew policeman were patroling the border.

"How close will they come to these bushes?" Mother asked, very frightened.

On the other side of the river, lay West Germany and freedom. There we saw people acting strangely, as though doing exercises.

Hans and Peter looked long at the people across the river, as though wanting to make sure of something. Then they said to us, "They are not doing exercises. They are only pretending. They are really helping people across the river. Let's signal to them to help us."

The two boys signaled that we wanted to cross. In answer, an elderly man came paddling toward us, standing on a board about the size of a small table, perhaps three feet by four feet. As he neared us we could see a rope at both ends of the board.

"My name is Franz," the man said. "We have to work quickly. Only one person at a time can sit on that board with a piece of luggage."

We looked at the board. We looked at the river. We could not swim. But there was no time to waste. Mother volunteered to go first. I cautioned, "Mother, don't look at the water. You might get dizzy and tumble in."

Franz took hold of the spool of rope at his end. The other end was held by someone on the other side of the river who would now pull by winding it up as it unwound on this side. When Mother stepped on shore ten minutes later, Franz pulled the board back for the next one.

Waiting until last, I watched my family being pulled over, one by one. For each one I trembled in fear and prayed in faith. The roaring motorcycles behind me reminded me of the angry officer who had put us in prison. If he knew we were out of prison now and were crossing the river to the West, I was sure he would have us killed.

"How wide is this river?" I asked Franz while waiting for my turn.

"About 400 feet" he replied.

"If police would find you here, would you be in trouble also?"

"Oh, yes, my Fraulein. I probably would be put in prison or maybe even shot, but I love to help people. Last night someone was shot while he tried to swim across."

I could tell that this helpful friend was suffering much fear.

"Thank you for helping us," I told him simply.

My turn to cross the river came, then his. With the protecting hand of our dear Lord, all of us made it across safely, including Hans and Peter. From the depth of our hearts, we thanked those dear people who risked their lives for us, though our appreciation was far beyond what words were able to express.

Our family looked at each other and said, "Another miracle has taken place for us. Only God kept the guards from coming by while we were crossing the river." We could say with the Psalmist: "Trust in him at all times; ye people, pour out your heart before him: God is a refuge for us" (Psalm 62:8).

"Now you are free," Franz told us. "You are in West Germany."

NOW YOU ARE FREE! FREE! These words sounded too good to believe. We felt as though we were starting a brand new page of our life.

I was reminded of Mr. and Mrs. Helbert. If they had come with us, they would have been safe in West Germany also.

As we stood there looking back across the river, we could still hear the roar of the motorcycles. But we had no fear of them now. We were out of their reach.

With fear gone, our bodies began to make their needs known. We felt extreme thirst.

"May we have a drink of water?" we asked Franz.

Franz and his helpers gave us cool water to drink. Mother gave us all some of the cake she had left. How we enjoyed those refreshments in the cool of the evening in the land of freedom.

I noticed Mother looking at the river with tears rolling down her face. I asked, "Mother, are you all right?"

"Yes, Lilli, I am overwhelmed with thankfulness which I cannot really explain."

"Mother," Ida spoke up, "our heavenly Father watched over us each step of our way. We are not alone."

Still watching the river, and still deeply moved, Mother continued. "I am very thankful to have my three children with me in the land of freedom, but how much more important it is when we cross the river into eternity, that we are ready, that we have our sins forgiven, that we might be clothed in white. When Jesus stands on the other side of the river and welcomes us home, I want to be able to say, 'Lord, here I am, and my three children which you have given me.'"

"How many miles is it to the railroad station?" Mother asked.

"It is six miles," Franz told us.

After resting a while, we picked up our luggage and began to walk to the railroad station. Walking seemed a pleasure now. Our feet were free, stepping on free soil. Scenery looked more beautiful now. We saw it through free eyes. Even people looked different. We no longer felt them eyeing us suspiciously, guessing we were runaways. Praise God, we were free!

We began to lag, however, partly because we wanted to enjoy everything as we went, and partly because our bodies were exhausted.

Peter and Hans urged us to walk faster. Though we found this difficult, we quickened our steps the best we could.

Unspeakable gratitude welled up within us as we reached that railroad station in West Germany. Just four hours earlier, in East

Germany, the police had taken us off the train.

Now we no longer needed to be afraid. We freely walked into the depot and bought tickets to Stade, a depot near where Erika lived. We needed to buy tickets for Peter and Hans also, since no one was allowed to stay in the depot overnight without a ticket.

We spent the night sitting on the floor. Though this was our second night of sitting on a floor, we made no complaint. Mother expressed our feelings well when she asked, "Isn't this much easier than being in prison or being in fear?"

We helped pass the time by reviewing our recent experiences.

I asked Peter, "Would you please explain to us those boards that brought us across the river? They floated on the top of the water. Were they really just boards nailed together? I could not see anything else."

"No," Peter replied, "the men had five-gallon gas cans fastened underneath. The cans were empty, and tightly sealed. They kept the boards on top of the water."

"Oh . . . now I understand. Then it was the five-gallon gas cans that brought us to freedom?"

"Yes."

"Five-gallon gas cans, besides Franz, the river, and rope," I added.

"But why was the raft so small?"

Hans answered, "So it could not be seen from the other side."

"It was frightening," Mother could not help saying. "If our papa could have been with us, maybe he would have found another way for us to come to West Germany."

Morning came and our train arrived. Peter and Hans helped us with our luggage. We paid them, thanked them for their help, and bade them good-by.

In our hearts we also thanked God for Franz, river, rope, and gas cans. With these He had brought us into freedom.

VIII

FREEDOM WITH CLOSED DOORS

"Stade!" called the conductor, bringing our two-hour train ride to an end. We made our way to Erika's house, where a happy reunion took place. We had not seen each other for four years. Now, together once more, we sang and prayed and shared the great love of Jesus.

We learned fast that we were in a new country, especially when it came to food. In order to acquire ration cards here, we had to be registered. In order to be registered we needed a place to live.

Before we arrived, Erika had received a telegram from the mission with which she had put us in touch while still at Aunt Frederika's. The telegram stated they would help us find a place to live.

Erika lived in a rented room on a farm, however. And this being harvest time, the farmer needed help in his fields. Since we had no West German ration cards and could not buy food, we gladly stayed for a week and worked. Afterwards, the farmer told us, Erika would be free to go with us to the mission and introduce us there.

The mission was located in Kassel, West Germany. Erika told us, however, about a border line near Kassel, over which no one could cross without a British Identification Card.

"Now what can we do?" Mother asked. "I thought we were free. Is there no resting place for us poor wanderers?"

Erika had an idea. She would borrow identification cards for all of us, travel with us to Kassel, then return the cards to the owners.

This didn't seem right to me. I asked Erika, "Is there no other way? What will happen to us if we are caught?"

Erika knew of no other way. We had to get to Kassel to accept the help offered us. So, feeling both fearful and helpless, we said yes to Erika.

Erika borrowed four identification cards for us, and the next morning we prepared to leave. The farmer for whom Erika worked hitched his horses to his wagon to take us to the train depot.

We said good-by to his family and climbed onto the wagon, Erika with us.

On the train we sat very quietly, afraid to talk for fear our conversation would be overheard. We hardly felt free to pray either, because of guilt about those passports. And the nearer we came to the border, the more our fear increased.

At 1:00 in the morning, we reached the

border depot. Everyone had to leave the train for inspection. Our identification cards were inspected by two officers standing on either side of the door. One officer asked my sister her name. She was so frightened that she forgot her assumed name. The other officer said, "Just let her go. She is too sleepy."

From a safe distance Mother gasped, "What would we have done if Ida had been caught? As though answering her own question, she reasoned, "We all would have had to surrender."

"God had His hand over us in spite of our wrongdoing," I said, my heart still pounding with fear.

Thankful and relieved that we had reached Kassel, we tried to put our fears away. Here in this town was the mission from which we had received the telegram. "Now," we thought, "everything will be all right. They promised to help us find a place to live."

At the mission, however, they told us they were not able to do anything for us.

"Then why did they send us that telegram saying they would help us?" Mother lamented to the rest of us, unable to understand such procedure on the part of a Christian mission.

We looked at each other helplessly. Erika turned to me and said, "I know these people in the mission very well, but I didn't know they would promise help when they could not help."

We thought of the many frightening hours traveled on borrowed passports in order to reach this mission. Now must our hopes be shattered?

After more discussion with the mission personnel, we were referred to Bahnhof's Mission in Bebra, a two-hour train ride from Kassel. There, they told us, a representative from their mission would help us.

With new hope we prayed together with Erika, asking the Lord to be with us, and to give us the guidance we needed. We thanked Erika for all the help she had given us, said good-by to her, and watched her take the next train back to Stade.

Now we felt very much alone in a strange country.

We took the train to Bebra and found Bahnhof's Mission. It was a train depot mission, something like a rescue mission in North America, equipped with a kitchen and beds. The mission offered each occupant one bowl of noodle soup per day and a bed with a mattress which was a gunny sack filled with straw.

We met with the representative from the Kassel mission. He told us that the government of that part of Germany had to stop receiving refugees. There weren't enough homes for them.

We told him, "We received a telegram from Kassel that you would help us."

"Last week I could have," he said with regret, "but this week it is too late."

"You mean we are one week too late?" I asked.

"Yes," he answered.

"Oh, why did we stay a week to help that farmer?" I lamented.

"But Lilli," Mother reminded me, "it was harvest time, and that farmer needed us as badly as we needed Erika to come with us."

What was left for us to do now? We had to be registered somewhere in order to get ration cards, or we would die of starvation.

We stayed at the mission three days, sleeping on straw-filled gunny sacks for mattresses and receiving one meal a day.

During those three days we repeatedly saw police come in and take refugees out.

I asked our representative, "What are the police doing with those refugees?"

He said, "They put them into buses and return them to East Germany."

My family and I kept praying silently.

"Will we have to go back also?" was Mother's worried question.

"But where would we go?" Ida asked. "Are there no other camps?"

I told myself we could not go back now, after all we had gone through to reach freedom. Again and again I prayed, "Dear Jesus, please help us. You are our Father in heaven. We know we have been led by Your hand this far."

Not one of those policemen ever ordered us out or even asked us why we were there. God must have blinded their eyes to us.

Once more I appealed to the mission representative. He went with me to the mayor of the town.

"Sorry," the mayor began his negative answer, "but I cannot help you this week. As you have already been told, we had to stop taking refugees. But there is a refugee camp at Allenberg. I can send you there."

What could I possibly say to the mayor? One week too late! Was there no mercy for us four wanderers? We were in a land of freedom with closed doors.

We arrived at Allenberg at midnight and found a very friendly refugee camp. They asked us how many blankets we needed for the night and gave us warm beds.

We could hardly believe these kindnesses were real. We thought how wonderful it would be if we could just stay there, for we were weary of wandering. Train travel had been crowded and uncomfortable; walking had been exhausting.

That night we began to wonder, "Would we have left Aunt Frederika's if we had known what all would happen to us? Were we free after all? We needed a place to live. We needed food. We needed love. We needed to be accepted. Can people need all these things and still be free?"

"What a beautiful town!" we all thought the next morning, seeing it by daylight.

The breakfast call sounded at 7:00.

Fritz spoke for all of us when he said, "I wonder what we will receive for breakfast."

Thankfully, we ate the bowl of oatmeal soup that made up our breakfast. "Can we pay for it?" Mother asked.

"Oh no, it is all free," the people in the kitchen replied.

Then we were called to the office.

"Dear Lord," I prayed silently, "What will happen to us now?"

We were told the mission was not allowed to keep us and were given tickets to Wardorf, one hour away by train.

Very discouraged, we walked back to the train depot we had just left the night before.

"God, show us what we should do," I prayed.

As though in answer to that prayer, the thought came to me that I should go back to Kassel one more time. Even though they could not help us before, maybe somehow they could advise us now.

Leaving the family at the Allenberg depot, I took the train back to Kassel.

At the Kassel mission, all they could do was feel sorry for me. I couldn't help wondering why the doors to a more solid future always seemed closed. Yet, I accepted this as a testing time that we had to go through, and I knew God had not taken His hand away from us.

On my way back to Allenberg I had to change trains. Close to the depot were ruins from bombings. During my five-hour layover, I cannot say how many times I ran behind those walls for prayer. There was no hope for human help any more. Somehow God had to do a miracle. In agony I poured out my heart to Jesus.

At midnight I realized I had not had food or drink since the breakfast of oatmeal soup. So fervently had I been praying for direction from the Lord that I was not aware of hunger or thirst.

As I returned from my praying, shortly before the arrival of my train, I saw a man with crutches sitting in the waiting room. He said to me in German, "I know you have not had anything to eat all day. Here, girl, take these ration cards to the little shop here in the station and buy some rolls for you and me."

I gladly obeyed, so moved I was unable to keep my tears back. God had not forgotten me. How great is His love and mercy! I had never seen that man before. God had sent him there just for me. Now I had something to eat.

Back in the Allenberg depot, I learned that my family had been fed miraculously also. They told me that people had brought them sandwiches without their asking. I thought of God's Word concerning Elijah: "And the ravens brought him bread and flesh in the morning, and bread and flesh in the evening; and he drank of the brook" (I Kings 17:6).

The next morning we took the train to

Wardorf, using the tickets that had been given us at the camp office in Allenberg.

On arriving in Wardorf, our greeting was a large sign outside the depot: "Refugees from East Germany have to go back."

We went into the depot praying, "Lord, we're looking for another miracle. We are at the end of our road."

After several hours in that depot, I noticed a boy about twelve years old watching us. A little later he came to us and asked kindly, "Don't you have a place to live?"

We told him our situation.

"Just come to our town," he invited.

"Where is it?" I asked, excited. "What is the name of the town?"

"Altenhunden," he answered. "It is a small town, but we have new people coming every week."

He told us how to get there and said we should talk to the mayor about a place to live.

"Shall we listen to him?" Mother asked with concern after the boy walked away from us.

I had bought train tickets for a town in the opposite direction. Erika had told us to try that town. If we listened to this boy, we would lose the money we had spent on the tickets.

I asked the ticket agent whether I could return our tickets and buy others to Altenhunden instead. He looked at me and said, "Girl, don't you know where you want to go?"

How could I tell him our situation? I kept

silent. Without any more questions, he took back the tickets I had bought, issued me new ones, and returned the leftover money to me.

"Praise the Lord!" I said in my heart.

"I feel so relieved," Mother said, sure now that we should take the boy's advice.

The train ride to Altenhunden lasted for several hours and took us through beautiful country.

While the family waited in the Altenhunden depot, I went to find the mayor. I found him in the midst of a public celebration. He showed me kind consideration. Though he could not take us into his town, he told me that the town of Siegen was still open to refugees.

Full of joy, I ran back to the depot.

"Mother!" I exclaimed. "The people in this part of Germany are very friendly and helpful. The mayor told me that we would be accepted in Siegen, a one-hour train ride from here."

I bought our tickets with joy. I also asked the agent if he would be so kind as to call the refugee camp at Siegen and see if they really would accept us. He called the camp and the answer was yes.

Mother's face brightened. "Will they really accept us?"

I said, "I hope so, Mother."

We took new courage. We felt new hope. And we used our three-hour wait for the Siegen train to reminisce once more.

"That mission in Kassel was not fair to us," Ida reasoned, "by sending us the telegram promising us help when really they could not help us at all. We had to go through so much fear with those borrowed passports, and I almost got caught when I couldn't think of my borrowed name."

"That is true, Ida," I agreed. "But the mission, I think, really couldn't help the change in the law. And about those passports, I didn't feel right about them at all."

"How long is it since we left Erika?" Mother asked.

"Seven days," I told her.

"Seven days?" Fritz repeated. "Seven is a perfect number in the Bible. That is why it took us seven days until we found a place where we will be accepted."

I shook my head. "Oh, no, Fritz, not really. We were tested and tried, and at the end of our testing, we shall come forth as gold."

On the train to Siegen, we met a friendly lady. I soon realized she had something in her hand that she wanted to shove into my pocket.

"Some money," she whispered. "You will need this."

"Thank you, lady." I was deeply moved by her kindness.

When we told her we were going to the refugee camp in Siegen, she said, "Oh, yes. I know where it is. I will go with you and show you the way. I can help with your luggage also."

Again we sensed God's leading. Night had fallen. There were no street lights in this war-bombed town. The half-hour walk to the camp would have been very difficult without help.

An overwhelming thankfulness which I cannot explain came over me. Even though the doors had so often been closed, God had been leading us all the while.

IX

AT MIDNIGHT

With grateful hearts we followed our new friend in the darkness to the Siegen refugee camp.

Police met us and took us into their quarters to disinfect us before allowing us to enter the camp.

"Will the camp accept us at this time of night?" we wondered.

"The staff in the office are still working," the officer told us. "I will try to talk to the manager through the loud speaker."

We heard him give our names and ages. After a short silence we could hear the manager answer, "Yes, we will take them. But remember, that is the last family we can take."

The officer took us through a gate into the camp area and on to the camp office.

Registration followed, requiring us to report at several offices in the camp. At the end of the process, I looked at the clock. Both hands pointed to twelve, and the date was August 2, 1947. It was a most wonderful midnight for us, one which we will always remember. On that particular midnight we became a part of the free world, and we felt praise in our hearts that we could not express.

After registration a lady from the office came to show us the way to the sleeping quarters—a large three-story building, dark now except where windows let in the bright moonlight. We followed her quietly, so as not to disturb the many sleeping people. After a while she opened a door to an empty room and said, "You can sleep here the rest of this night. Tomorrow morning the camp manager will get you all organized." Then she said goodnight and left.

For a few minutes we sat and talked in muffled voices.

"What would we have done," Mother asked, "if the camp manager would have changed his mind and would not have accepted us?"

"Yes, Mother," I had to agree, "our freedom depended on one man. If he had said no, there would have been no mercy. All other camps beyond this are closed. We would have had to go back to East Germany. What a terrible thought!"

"It was also a miracle," Fritz reminded, "that the little boy found us among all the people to tell us about Altenhunden."

"God is never late," I emphasized. "And He always does things in ways far beyond our understanding. We can trust Him in every circumstance."

Our room had triple-bunk, wooden beds.

The mattresses and pillows were made of burlap, filled with straw. This was so much better than the conditions in the prison and railroad stations. With a roof over our heads, with our wandering over, and with fear about being sent back to East Germany gone, anything looked good to us.

We woke up the next morning to the sound of many people stirring in the building. Fritz and Ida wanted to go for a walk, but we all needed to stay in our room until the manager met with us.

Soon a knock sounded on our door.

"*Guten Morgen* (good morning)," greeted the man to whom I opened the door.

"I am Mr. Litke, the camp manager. Did you have a good rest?"

"Oh, yes, Mr. Litke, we surely did, thank you."

"I suppose you are hungry. Shortly you may go to the kitchen to receive your week's supply of bread and jam. It is free."

"Free?" I asked in amazement. "Do you mean we get the food free?"

"Yes, as long as you live here in the camp you get everything free."

"How long do people stay here?" I wondered.

"About four or five weeks. It depends on the government—how fast they find rooms for you to move into. Now I want to show you your room, right across the hall here. It has twenty-eight people, and only four more empty beds. The four of you will fill every bed."

Mr. Litke opened the door and called in, "I have brought you four more guests."

"How many people are in this camp?" I asked.

"We are 1500."

"And how many buildings?" I pursued further.

"We have six large buildings. Now concerning your meals, you will receive some coffee in the morning and evening and a bowl of potato soup for lunch. It will be brought in milk cans and served in the hall. When the people get noisy in the hall, you will know it is lunch time. I must go now. Do you have any more questions?"

"No. Thank you so much."

We gathered our few belongings and put them on the beds since there were no chairs or tables.

Ida asked, "May I go now, Mother, to get that bread?"

"Yes, Ida, you may go."

The rest of us, with nothing else to do, sat on our beds.

We still could hardly believe that we were receiving bread from the West German government free. To us this was another miracle.

Suddenly we heard a commotion in the hall. People were rushing to get their potato soup. We counted it a privilege to join them.

While we sat on our beds eating our soup,

Ida returned from the kitchen with bread, jam, and butter.

Mother asked her, "How much bread do you have?"

"Four loaves of French bread, one loaf per person for a week; also two tablespoons of jam and one tablespoon of butter per person for a week."

We felt rich.

I looked at the bread and began calculating. "If we had other food to go with it, such as vegetables—! But just a loaf of bread per person a week! We'll have to make little marks on the loaves and figure how much we dare cut each day. If we eat too much one day, by the end of the week we will be without bread."

We still had some money left that we had not spent for traveling, but we had not yet acquired West German ration cards, and without them we could not buy food. Mother, however, assured us, "I know we will not die of starvation in this camp."

She took out our precious Bible, the one we had found on the street, and read my favorite verse. "Commit thy way unto the Lord; trust also in him; and he shall bring it to pass" (Psalm 37:5). She also read Psalm 125:1: "They that trust in the Lord shall be as mount Zion, which cannot be removed, but abideth for ever." Then she added, "The Word of God has been such a comfort and guideline for our lives."

One thing bothered Mother a great deal,

however. She said, "If we only knew for sure that the East German government has given our cousin Selma those 1000 marks we borrowed from her, then everything would be all right."

"That reminds me, Mother," I almost interrupted. "We must write to Aunt Frederika and give her our address. They promised to let us know when they received the money."

At Siegen I felt handicapped over the lack of privacy, as I loved to be alone with God in prayer. Then I discovered steps in our building that led to an attic. Many times I went up there to pray. Frequently I found other Christians there also, praying. Sometimes we prayed together. Always we encouraged each other and promised to remember each other in our prayers.

The buildings of the refugee camp stood on a hill outside the town of Siegen, which lay in a valley. The scenery was beautiful, except for the war scars. Many, many ruins still remained from the bombings and destruction two years earlier.

Although I wanted a job, nobody was permitted to find employment before having a place to live. I was not used to just walking around or sitting on beds. I missed my hymnbooks and guitar. The only songbook I had was one I had handwritten from memory. The time went slowly for us.

Mother's uneasiness about the 1000 borrowed marks continued. Frequently she said to me, "What will we do if Selma doesn't receive that money from the government? We have it nearly all spent on traveling. You have already signed the statement that we have received it, but we are not there to make sure she is reimbursed."

"Don't worry, Mother," I begged. "God will take care of it. I wrote to Irene, Selma's sister-in-law, as soon as we were accepted here in this camp. Surely she will answer my letter as soon as she gets it."

Two weeks passed without mail for us. I went for walks or climbed into the attic to talk to God about it. I was almost sure Selma would receive the money. I felt that God had it all planned for us.

Finally a letter came from Irene. "The one we've been waiting for!" I told myself excitedly as I opened it and began to read.

"Mother!" I called, "they did receive the money without any problem. And listen to this. Irene says, 'And the government gave your family almost twice as much as it gave to other refugees.'"

We praised the Lord in both joy and relief. One thousand German marks was a lot of money. It would have taken us a long time to pay that amount back to Selma had the government not done so.

"Why did I worry?" Mother rebuked herself. "I should have trusted the Lord to meet all our needs."

I continued reading from Irene's letter.

"Three weeks after you left we heard a knock on our door. When we opened it, there stood Mr. Alexander! We told him we thought he had left the country with the potatoes and butter, and that after you waited for him three weeks, you left with somebody else.

"Mr. Alexander explained to us that he had been sick and had not been able to come sooner. When he asked about your welfare, we told him you were put in prison three times but that you are safe."

"I wonder," Mother thought out loud, "if Mr. Alexander was a Christian."

After receiving the letter, we were more relaxed at Siegen, but we still had needs. One of them was Christian fellowship.

I began looking for a church to attend. One day while walking along the streets in Siegen I met a girl named Anna, a Christian who loved Jesus with all her heart. She was just the person I needed. Though she had never been a refugee, she knew the horrors of war. She had experienced tragedies in Siegen—bombings, loss of thousands of lives, and nerve-wracking fears which still lingered on. Her mother, among many others, suffered psychological wounds from which she probably never would recover.

Anna told me about the Salvation Army,

which I had never heard of before and invited me to go with her to a meeting. I gladly accepted, and felt such blessing at the service that I kept on going with her.

On Sunday afternoon the Salvation Army held street meetings, marching through the city, singing and playing instruments, stopping here and there where audiences would gather to hear their testimonies. Listeners sometimes joined in the testimony meeting, telling what God meant to them. The march ended at the Salvation Army headquarters, where all who wished entered for another service.

I rejoiced to see the Gospel proclaimed on the streets of this large city, and to witness the power of God in lives. I also rejoiced to have a Christian friend like Anna. We became close companions and were strengthened together in our faith.

Seven weeks went by. Although the manager of the camp had estimated our stay to be four or five weeks until the government found rooms for us, it became evident to us that rooms were becoming harder and harder to find. We were told that every room in West Germany was registered by the government. Any owner having one or more empty rooms had to make them available to families without homes. Refugees in our camp were allowed to choose between a room on a farm or a room in a city. Our family desired to go to a farm, feeling that food would be more plentiful there.

We waited and prayed. Finally the day came when 150 of us from the camp were told to get ready to move. Everything had been arranged for us, and an officer would go along.

We were transported by trucks to the train depot in Siegen where we boarded the train to Soest, a city smaller than Siegen. It had no ruins at all, and it lay in the midst of a beautiful farming area.

We were placed in a large school building, used as a refugee camp. Our food here was the same as at the Siegen camp. Our beds were piles of straw on the floor. With no bunk beds to climb, at least we were in no danger of falling out.

As the first week went by in our schoolhouse camp, we all became more and more anxious about what would happen to us. Would we be placed with friendly farmers? Many in the group seemed very discouraged. Plainly, we were unwanted people. The West Germans were giving their rooms to refugees only because they were forced to do so.

The reluctance of the West German people was understandable. Food was scarce, and already there were too many people.

In our helplessness we prayed much. Behind the building in a field were some trees and stumps. I can still recall sitting on those stumps and pouring out my heart to God for another miracle. "We are crushed, Lord," I told Him, "from all the fear and destruction of

137

war. Will You bring us to a friendly farmer?"

After several weeks in this camp, we saw a truck stop in front of our building and a government officer with the driver called out names of several families, including ours. We were given a short time to pack our few belongings and put them onto the truck.

We said good-by to the refugees remaining at the camp and boarded the truck. We felt rather like cattle as we were delivered to the places where we would live, one family being dumped off here and another there. We were thankful that the officer at least made sure the families were accepted by the farmers to whom they were assigned.

My family and I were the last ones on the truck. As we entered a small town, the officer said to us, "Here we are. This is Einecke, the town where we have a room for you."

My heart beat fast. The thought came to me, "What if the farmer says no? Will we have to go back to the school again?"

I asked the officer if he would come with us to the house. Thank God, he did.

Without saying a word, we all walked together to the house. The officer rang the doorbell and all four of us stood silently behind him with our few belongings in our hands.

"I brought you a family, Mr. Selzer," he told the farmer. "I know you have an empty room."

Mr. Selzer said nothing. Knowing he had

no choice, I felt sorry for him. He had to take us into his home.

I thanked the officer for coming along to the house. I felt thankful to the West German government also for helping us find a place to live. And as we moved into that room we all felt grateful for that special midnight hour, nine weeks before this, when our names were written in the West German books and freedom became ours.

X

ONE ROOM

Though Mr. Selzer said little that first night, he really was a friendly, large-hearted man. He showed us to our little eleven-by-eleven-foot room on the second floor. He already had a little wood stove in it, and he offered to sell us some of his own furniture. We had to carry water from the well and gather wood ourselves from a woods about a mile away. But that did not bother us. We thanked God for answering our prayers for a pleasant place to live and for this kind farmer.

We could not express in words what it meant to us to have a room all by ourselves. For two and one-half years we really had not belonged anywhere. We had lived with so many people together and had taken turns cooking our meals. Now at last that was over.

Now, we could register with the government and get ration cards. We had to go to Soest, sixteen kilometers from Einecke, to register.

"But how will we get there?" we wondered.

Mr. Selzer, whom we soon began calling Grandpa Henry, told us we would need to walk three miles to a railroad station, then take the train the remaining seven miles. He gave me directions to help me know where to walk and where to get off the train.

The next day I made my way to Soest. I had to go to several different offices, and to the police, to get our registering done. Without difficulty I found every office, and said to myself, "Praise the Lord."

After completing our registration, I received our ration cards. It gave me a grand feeling of independence to walk into the grocery store on my way home and buy some food. Even though I could not get very much food with the ration cards, I could walk with new morale and confidence. We now belonged to West Germany, we had a place to live, we were registered, and we had ration cards.

Through this time we never could forget Papa. We longed to have him with us here in our first home. Home was just not the same without him. Was he suffering in some prison camp? "O Lord," we prayed, "please help him."

We also wondered where our sister Marie and her family might be. And Mother's sister Amalie—was she still alive?

We wrote to the Red Cross asking them to relay news to us if our relatives could be located.

Fritz and Ida found good jobs, but I could not take a steady job because of Mother's poor health. I kept our household in order.

When potato harvest time came, we were given ration cards to buy potatoes. But when I brought our small allotment of potatoes home and placed them in Mr. Selzer's basement for storage, I realized those few potatoes would not last us for the whole year. Some of the farmers told me that after harvest I could pick up the potatoes left in the fields, since they would go to waste otherwise. Sugar beet farmers allowed us to glean also. Since sugar was scarce, we made syrup from sugar beets.

Gleaning potatoes and sugar beets made me feel as though I were living in Bible times. I thought especially of Ruth gleaning in the fields of barley and wheat.

It was kind of farmers to let me pick leftover potatoes and beets free. But I felt embarrassed walking to the fields to pick. I had to do it, though, or we would not have had enough to eat. We had money to buy, but farmers were not allowed to sell us any produce.

Picking those potatoes and beets was fairly easy work. It did not take long to fill my sack. Carrying them the three or four miles to our room was the tiresome part. They became heavier and heavier, and I had to pray for strength to reach home. I could not keep from crying sometimes, and thinking, "Why? Why?" Had we really needed the war? We had lost our home through war. We had lost our dear papa through war. Now I had to go to fields and pick up potatoes and sugar beets in order to have enough to eat, all because of war.

Then I thought of promises in the Bible. I felt them speaking directly to me in a still small voice. "Be of good courage, and he shall strengthen your heart, all ye that hope in the Lord" (Psalm 31:24).

"Yes, Lord," I prayed, "You have always strengthened me and You have always heard my cry. I will always be thankful. Please forgive me for asking why." Then I could feel peace and joy in my soul.

I was reminded of a beautiful poem that made a deep impression on my life. The poem described a Christian traveler with a cane in his hand and a heavy cross on his back, making his way to the Golden City. After walking in the heat of the day, he became very tired. Suddenly, he spied a saw.

Thinking about the long, heavy cross on his back, he told himself, "If I could cut off a piece, the cross would be lighter and I would get to the city more quickly." And so he did.

Soon he came in sight of the beautiful city. But as he came closer, he saw there was a stream between him and the city, with no bridge for crossing.

Then he thought, "How about the cross on my back? Could it not be used for a bridge?" He tried, but the cross was too short.

There he stood looking at the beautiful city but unable to enter.

"It is my fault," he wept. "I thought my

cross was too long and too heavy to carry."

Meanwhile, another traveler came, took his cross from his back, laid it across the stream, and walked triumphantly to the Golden City.

The traveler said to himself, "Perhaps I can use his cross to reach that city also." But when he stepped on the cross, it broke.

As I thought of that poem, I prayed, "Please, Father, forgive me for asking, 'Why?' Help me to take my cross as a gift from day to day, and count it as a blessing. Then someday it will bridge the stream to the Golden City, and I will stand before Jesus who bore His cross for me."

Harvest time ended. I looked at my big pile of potatoes in the basement bin. I looked at the jugs of syrup, and I was thrilled. I felt rich. We had very little bread and meat, but we could make various kinds of meals with those potatoes.

We were a happy, thankful family. We loved our little room. It was our kitchen, dining room, living room, and bedroom. We made it as comfortable and livable as possible. Just outside in the hall, Mr. Selzer arranged a little place for a twin bed where Fritz could sleep. His kindness was such a blessing.

One day while I was shopping in town, I felt a tap on my shoulder. I looked around and there was Mrs. Schulte, whom we had learned to know as a fellow refugee at camp.

Surprised and pleased to see her, I asked,

"Do you have a nice room?"

"Oh, no. I am still living in the school building."

"Why?" I asked.

"The government has not found a room for me yet," she answered sadly. "Did you get a nice room? And how is your mother?"

"We have a nice little room," I was glad to tell her, "and the family is very friendly. My mother is fine. Mrs. Schulte, God has been so good to us."

I tried to comfort the poor woman, but I felt rather helpless.

When I told my family at home about Mrs. Schulte, all were deeply moved.

"God is really good to us," Fritz remarked.

Ida agreed. "We have a place to live and have enough potatoes and sugar beet syrup. It means so much not to have to suffer hunger."

With life becoming more settled, we began looking for a church to attend. In testifying about Jesus to people I met on the streets and in grocery stores, I sometimes mentioned that I was trying to find a good church or prayer meeting. One day I learned that three miles from Einecke some people had a Bible study in their home.

The following Sunday I walked to the home and found there a small, friendly group.

We had a Bible study and then knelt for prayer. My heart was so full of praise that I was the first to pray.

After dismissal one lady said to me, "Didn't

you know that the women are to be silent in this prayer meeting?"

I blushed with surprise and shock. Never had I heard anything like that before. I told her I was very sorry; I did not know that was their belief.

On my return home Mother and Ida asked, "How was the prayer meeting?"

When I told them, they too were surprised.

"What are we going to do for fellowship," Ida asked. "Are there no other good churches to find anywhere?"

Again we missed our papa. If he were with us, surely he could find some group of believers with whom we could profitably fellowship.

Some weeks later I went to that Bible study again. This time they had a guest minister. After the service they invited me to stay for a cup of coffee. While we sat around sipping coffee, the minister took out his pipe and began to smoke, saying, "After a service my pipe always tastes good."

Never had I seen a minister smoking a pipe. Too disappointed to stay any longer, I said good-by and went home.

Now what? Our family longed for a spiritual church to attend. God had been good to us in letting us come to a land of freedom, but we needed fellowship with other Christians.

We began visiting a church four miles from Einecke. The large stone structure with its high bell tower sounded its invitation for miles around. Many people lived in that area, and the building could have been packed. Sad to say, we found only a few older men and women present.

This scant attendance was hard for us to understand, and the church did not meet our needs. Although the bells from its tower sounded out beautifully, to us that beauty was hollow.

We kept on looking for a church. Finally we found one that met our need. There we had good fellowship and found rich blessings. However, attending there meant traveling by train one hour each Sunday. This we could not do every week, so occasionally we still went to the church with the bells, and also to the home Bible study, but we had to remember not to pray out loud.

Several months went by. I thought about Mrs. Bauman, the lady I had met after church when we were still living with Aunt Frederika. Mother thought about her too, and kept saying, "I wonder if Mrs. Bauman has kept her promise and has sent our address to her relatives in Canada."

"Surely mail will be coming soon," I reasoned. "Wouldn't it be exciting to receive mail from Canada again?"

Ida said, "I'm sure Mother's cousins in the United States of America would write if they read our address."

One day a letter arrived from Aunt Frederika, and in it we found a letter from

Grandma. It was our first word from Canada. Reading it brought tears of joy. Mrs. Bauman had kept her promise to us. God had worked another miracle.

Several days later a letter came from a cousin of Mother's in the United States. This, like the letter from Grandma, brought joy to our hearts and hope for our future. Perhaps the day would come when we could immigrate to America.

About the same time as the letters arrived, we learned we had been among the very first to fill out forms applying for immigration to America. This indicated we might be among the first ones to immigrate.

Soon we began receiving help from relatives in Canada and the United States. Parcels came that were plainly packed with love. They contained beautiful clothing and unperishable foods such as rice, noodles, and coffee. Gratefully, we knelt to thank God for providing so abundantly.

Life became easier for us. We were well dressed again, we were able to save enough money to buy new bicycles for us three children, and we had a variety of food to eat with our potatoes. We were rich.

Now we could also afford to make our room a little more cozy and pretty. We decorated it with pink and blue wall paper. We painted the woodwork white and the floor brown. We put curtains on our little windows.

In the hall outside our room was a wooden

clothes closet. Mr. Selzer let us use one side of that closet to hang our beautiful American clothes.

Although we had the most needed things, we still had an unsatisfied desire. We wanted to immigrate to America. Three years had come and gone since our move to our one-room home. Those were three character-building years. We were taught many things concerning patient waiting and praying for the Lord's direction. But we wanted a home of our own, and we believed we could have that in America sooner than in Germany. Still, we wanted God's will above our own.

Friends and neighbors frequently asked us, "Why do you want to go to America? You have everything you need here in Germany." Did they not know that many of the things we had came from America? That we would have remained poor except for the help from America?

We learned about Church World Service, an organization in the United States, that helped people with their immigration procedures. They did a wonderful job in managing things for us.

After preliminary details were cared for, we received permission to immigrate to America, providing we could get American sponsors. These sponsors would need to take financial responsibility for our transportation to America and for our living accomodations there, so we would not be a burden to the American government.

Our family shrank from asking our relatives in America to sponsor us. They had already been helping us much. How could we put them to more trouble?

We talked to our heavenly Father and asked Him what to do. We felt His approval on our planning for immigration, but we wondered how to find a sponsor.

"I have three cousins in the U.S.A.," Mother reminded us. "Which one do you think we should ask?"

"Uncle George," Ida thought out loud. Although he was a cousin, we children called him uncle. "I am sure he would be willing to help us."

I nodded. "I think so too. He always writes nice, kind letters."

We all agreed on Uncle George, and Mother said, "Lilli, you must write today."

"Yes, Mother," it was fairly easy for me to say. Picking up the pen and paper, however, was extremely difficult. It took tears and prayers and courage for me to write Mother's cousin and his dear wife, Mr. and Mrs. George Buchholz in Portland, Oregon, asking if they would be so kind as to sponsor our family. I promised that we would be willing to do our best at any kind of job.

Asking the Lord to have His way, I mailed the letter.

Several weeks went by. Mother frequently asked, "If Uncle George cannot sponsor us, what are we going to do?"

"The Lord has always found a way for us," we children told her, "and He will not fail us this time."

Finally the letter came. With mixed feelings I opened the letter and began to read. Soon I burst out, "Mother, Uncle George is willing to sponsor three of us. And he has a friend named Ganke who is in need of a girl to help with their housework. They offered to sponsor Ida."

Deeply moved, and almost speechless, we had to let our inner feelings express our gratefulness to God and these sponsors. There were many tears of joy. Only a person who has gone through what we did can fully understand what I mean by tears of joy.

I was reminded of the verse, "When thou passest through the waters, I will be with thee; and through the rivers, they shall not overflow thee: when thou walkest through the fire, thou shalt not be burned; neither shall the flame kindle upon thee" (Isaiah 43:2).

With the burden of finding sponsors lifted, we began more definite plans for immigration. The legal aspects took a long time. We often felt discouraged by the many delays, and had to pray for patience.

During our wait of almost a year, we were invited for an interview with the American consul in Duesseldorf, West Germany, a two-hour train trip for us.

It made us happy to know at least they were

still working on our immigration papers and we were not forgotten. Ida and Fritz took time off from work, and all of us went by train.

"What would we learn?" we wondered nervously. We had been told the U.S.A. was a rich country where people were able to buy a house in a short time if they worked hard. "And what about language?" We spoke only German. Would the consul understand us? Inwardly I prayed for help.

As we entered the office, we were amazed at the friendliness of the American consul and at the beautiful German he spoke. He listened very carefully, then said to me, "When you arrive in the United States of America, be sure to write a book about your life story. I am sure people will be very interested in reading it."

On the way home we talked excitedly about that gracious American consul.

"But he did not tell us how much longer we have to wait," Fritz said.

Ida spoke up. "But he was so nice and friendly. If he had known, he surely would have told us."

We decided, judging from him, that American people must all be nice, generous, good-hearted people.

"And judging from all the clothing and food our churches have received to hand out to German people in need," I added, "there must be no other country like it. Won't it be wonderful to live in a country like that?"

Several months after our visit with the American consul we received an invitation to camp Wendorf for an examination both physically and politically. To immigrate to America we would need to be in good health and free from any Nazi belief or activism. We were told in the invitation that the examination would probably take two weeks. Our meals and lodging would be furnished free.

Happy over the prospects ahead now, we packed needed things and boarded the train.

Mother, as usual, had misgivings and fears. Losing Papa and never hearing what happened to him had left lasting scars on her. "It sounds frightening," she commented. "Two weeks for an examination! What will we do if we aren't accepted?"

"Mother," I reminded her, "we have prayed much about it. If it is the Lord's will, we will be accepted."

During those two weeks in Wendorf, I met Greta, a Christian girl who shared her life story with me.

Learning that she, like us, had escaped from East Germany, I told her that my mother had a sister, Amalie Kitzman, somewhere in East Germany. I told her that since our escape we had lost track of her, though we were sure she had had to escape also.

When I mentioned the town, Greta looked at me in stunned surprise and exclaimed, "Lilli, Amalie Kitzman was my neighbor! I used to live in that city."

It was my turn to exclaim. "Greta! Please come with me to my mother! She will be so happy to hear about her sister."

Excited, we hurried to Mother, and Greta told us all about Aunt Amalie. Then she added, "And I have her address at home. I will gladly send it to you if you give me your address."

I quickly wrote it down for her.

Aunt Amalie was a Christian. Her only daughter had died at nineteen. I was sure she prayed much that somehow God would perform a miracle so we could hear from each other again. Now that miracle was taking place. I realized anew that God has everything planned for our lives. I could never have found Greta if I had tried. God had brought us together.

Our examination went perfectly, and we were given all the necessary papers for immigration. Then we were told to go home and wait until we were called to board the ship.

We went home a happy family.

Several days later the mailman brought us a letter from Greta, containing Aunt Amalie's address. Now, after many years, Mother could have the joy of writing to her sister again.

Not long after this we had another surprise. We heard voices in the hall, and I went out to see who was there. A policeman had come up the stairs with his German shepherd police dog on a leash.

"I came to see you," he said pleasantly.

Taking him to our room, we answered his questions and told him our story. He advised us to be patient a little longer, saying, "If you remain healthy you probably will immigrate soon. Good luck to you."

In my excitement I never asked him by whom he was sent nor why he had come. But I was not worried. We had not done anything that we knew of that could hinder our immigration.

Next morning I met our mayor in passing. With a smile he said, "Last night a policeman came to see me. He asked me all about your family."

Again, I did not have the courage to ask the mayor what the policeman was asking about us.

Mail came from everywhere, among it two very special letters.

The first letter notified us that we were scheduled to board a ship named *Greely* early in October, for our departure to America.

The second letter came from Aunt Amalie. We thanked God that it came promptly, while we were still in Germany. As we supposed, she had many needs. Remembering our year of privation with Aunt Frederika, we could easily guess what these needs might be. We were glad we had enough time to pack some food and clothing to send to her.

Before we were permitted to leave Germany, I had to go to many government offices and give them information about our leaving.

October came. We did our final packing. We ate our last meal in the little room that had been our home for more than four years. Finally, we knelt for prayer, thanking God for all the blessings and kindnesses we had received in West Germany and giving ourselves into His care for the future.

Grandpa Henry prepared his horse and wagon for us. We loaded our luggage. With thankful hearts and tear-filled eyes, we said good-by to Grandpa's wife and large family, along with the friendly neighbors who had gathered to see us off. Then we stepped on the wagon and Grandpa Henry took us to the train depot.

This was our final train ride in West Germany. It seemed like a dream to us. I said to Mother, "Can you believe we are on our way to America?"

"Yes," she answered, "I can. I thank God for it. We have prayed and waited for over five years—ever since our stay with Aunt Frederika began."

Fritz, typical boy, said, "It is good we are being sent to the same camp where we had our examination. I hope the boys I met will still be there."

Arriving at the camp, we all looked for the friends we had met before. Sure enough, they were all there. That made Fritz and the rest of us very happy.

We found ourselves among thousands of

people at Camp Wendorf waiting to immigrate to America. Here all luggage was marked, all people were counted and listed, and all last-minute legal proceedings were taken care of. Then we were all transported to Grohn, near the Bremer seaport, where we would board the *Greely* for the United States of America.

During those last days in Germany, our thoughts tossed from present to past to future. Sometimes they centered around our little room at Grandpa Henry's. That room had sheltered us through many highs and lows of our free life in West Germany. It had become home to us. In a way it was hard to leave. On the other hand, uncramped room awaited us in America, and our thoughts raced ahead to meet it. With the Lord's help, we meant to face the beckoning future.

XI

AMERICA THE BEAUTIFUL

We found Grohn to be a small camp, and very different from Wendorf. It was completely under American control. The buildings were new. The food was very good and very plentiful. Most of us had never seen so much good food before. In many ways we felt we were already in a different country.

One outstanding experience at Grohn I will always remember. I saw men marching to the mast on which the American flag was fastened. The flag was slowly lowered while through the loud speaker came that beautiful song, one line of which was, "America, America, God shed His grace on thee."

I had never seen or heard anything like that before. Unable to understand English, I got only two of the words, *America* and *God,* but they were enough for me. I told myself that America must be a Christian nation. Deeply touched, I let my tears flow. My life was turning to a fresh new day. Bright sunshine was showing through the clouds, and I did not know how I could thank God enough for everything.

Full of expectancy, we waited. What would we find on reaching the U.S.A.? Would the people be friendly? Would there be any poor people like us?

No one seemed to be worried about the language problem, even though we could not speak English. So we did not think much about it either. All we were excited about was seeing the United States of America.

Our wait at Grohn lasted a week, but the time did not seem long. We enjoyed every minute. The food was always good, and the hospitality warm and kind. And each morning and evening, we were thrilled to listen to the song, "America the Beautiful," as it came over the loud speaker.

When the *Greely* arrived, we were told to board ship. This announcement brought us added happiness and excitement.

Everything was so well organized, and directions were so clear, that we all knew what to do. The *Greely*, a warship, had not been built for families, so women were sent to one end of the boat and men to the other. Everyone cooperated gladly, no one complained, and although there were over a thousand of us, we found our places quickly.

Joyous chatter sounded everywhere among us. We were on our ship at last, ready to cross the ocean for America.

About an hour later we felt the boat slowly leaving the harbor. We were on our way!

"I hope I don't get seasick," Mother said, and others made similar expressions.

I had some songbooks with me that I had bought in West Germany. A group of us girls gathered together and sang.

"This is just great," I thought. "And I purposed to have more singing, Bible study, and prayer among us in the days ahead."

The first night at sea we hit a terrible storm. We women, in the forepart of the ship, had it the roughest. The men, bunking in the stern, felt less severe tossing. By morning most of us women were unable to walk. Again and again we heard cooks asking over the loud speaker for women to come and help in the kitchen. None of us felt able to go.

After four days the ocean grew quiet, and most of us felt well again. It was understood that we were to earn our fare to America by working. Besides helping in the kitchen, there were many other jobs for all who were able to work. Men painted. Women cleaned. I took care of the kindergarten department.

We all had to go to the dining room for our meals. Sometimes we had to stand in line and wait, but we were thankful for the good food. And it was all free!

The second week of our voyage turned out to be much more enjoyable than the first. With seasickness over and our bodies well again, we could do the work expected of us and have some pleasant leisure time besides.

My work in the kindergarten department

lasted several hours each day. Then I was free to go on deck, where I tried to find a little spot all to myself. Here I loved to watch the beautiful blue sky with its white, fluffy clouds, and the ocean beneath, now deep and quiet.

While I sat there all alone, my thoughts sometimes went back to some of the fearful moments I had known. I saw myself sitting on that three-by-four-foot board being pulled across the river by a rope when escaping from East Germany. It seemed as though I could still hear the roar of the motorcycles of the police patroling the border.

"Am I really on a big ship now?" I asked myself. "Am I really on my way to the United States of America?"

We didn't find time to sing together or have the Bible studies I had hoped to have. With seasickness and our little jobs occupying us, before we realized it we had been on the ocean for two weeks.

We could hardly believe our ears when the loud speaker announced, "We are landing at New Orleans, Louisiana, in the United States of America." We thanked God for a safe arrival, and got our luggage together for disembarking.

On our ship were refugees representing three religious groups—Jewish, Catholic, and Protestant, helped by several different agencies. To identify us we were given pins labeled with the initials of the agency which had helped us. Most Protestant refugees wore the letters C.W.S. (for Church World Service). All luggage had similar identification tags.

While we were leaving the ship, we were told to watch for a table with a large sign showing the same letters as those we were wearing. At that table we would pick up our tickets for inland travel.

After reporting at the ship's office once more, this time for our temporary alien registration cards, we were ready to go ashore. The boat's doors then opened ahead of us, and with thankful hearts we stepped onto American soil.

"Good-by to all of you," the ship's crew called out through the loud speaker. "Good luck in the United States."

The date was November 6, 1951.

Perhaps some who helped in the Church World Service at that time will read this little book. To you I would like to say, "Thank you from the depth of my heart for all you have done for us."

Also to the government of the United States of America, I say, "Thank you for bringing us to this country. May God bless America for all it has done and is still doing for people in need."

XII

A DIFFERENT WORLD

At last we had reached the United States of America! Our dreamland! The land about which people in Europe were saying, "Everyone is rich!"

As we came down from the ship into a large building, we found members of the Salvation Army waiting for us with donuts and coffee. What a kind, warm welcome! Our family wished we could at least have known how to say thank-you, but we could not speak one word.

After enjoying our donuts and coffee, we walked on, looking for the large C.W.S. sign. Finally we discovered it and made our way to that table where we received our train tickets to Portland, Oregon. These had been purchased by C.W.S. with money sent by our sponsors.

Soon a lady came to us and said, "My name is Miss Meier. I have been asked by Church World Service to take you in my car to the train depot."

It thrilled us to hear Miss Meier speak German. Her use of our language helped give us the confidence in her that we needed. It helped put us at ease among our many uncertainties.

Miss Meier not only took us to the train depot, but she also helped us read the big posted schedule of arriving and departing trains. She looked at our train tickets and explained to us the time of arrival and departure at each place where we would need to change trains on our way to Portland. She assured us that we need have no fear of getting lost or taking a wrong train, because at every station there would be a responsible person with a list of our names. This person would take good care of us and get us onto the right train.

How wonderful it seemed to us that everything should be arranged so well for us! And how grateful we were to Miss Meier for relieving us of so many worries!

After this kind lady told us good-by and wished us well, we still had several hours to wait for our train. I said to my family, "Now we are in the large city of New Orleans in the U.S.A. Since we have some time, let's go and see what a city in the U.S.A. looks like."

Leaving Mother with the baggage, Fritz, Ida, and I went for a walk.

We were almost unable to believe what we saw. Inside store windows things for sale were covered with dust. On the streets newspapers and other litter blew around in the breeze. What a disappointment to us! Everyone in the

U.S.A. was supposed to be rich. We wondered now where the rich people lived.

We returned to the depot and told Mother what we had seen. She tried to cheer us by telling us, "Living in America will be much better than living in one room in Germany."

A train came. We knew it was ours, and we started for it.

"Wait! Wait!" called a man, running toward us. "It is my job to help you."

Again we were surprised at the friendliness and helpfulness of the American people.

We had little to say while riding the train. We were busy with our thoughts and full of amazement at the sights we saw as we sped along.

According to our schedule, our first train change would be in Kansas City, Kansas. Miss Meier had made this clear to us, and had pointed it out to us on our tickets.

As we neared Kansas City, the conductor called it out and named connections passengers could make to various destinations. Also I saw the name on buildings and signs as I looked out through the window of our slowing train.

"We have to get off here," I said to my family as the train stopped. "Please hurry."

We grabbed our things and stepped off, excited and wondering. Never before had we experienced traveling in a country whose language we could not speak.

We walked into the Kansas City depot at

10:00 a.m. We would be leaving at 2:25 p.m. That would mean a wait of four hours and twenty-five minutes.

None of us felt like browsing around in this city. Unable to speak English, we might get lost. Instead we entertained ourselves by watching the many people come and go. How differently they dressed in the U.S.A. In Germany elderly ladies always wore black or navy blue clothes, especially in winter. Here we saw women of any age in almost any color. And men! We had never seen men in bright yellow or bright red hats in Germany.

Several hours went quickly by and we began wondering how we would find our next train. We did not need to wonder long. A lady came, carrying a slip of paper with our names. Calling our names from her list, she asked us to come with her. She took us to our train and helped us on. By this time we had learned how to word a thank-you in English, and it gave us great satisfaction to tell her good-by and thank her for her help.

When we were on our way again, I took out my schedule and said to my family, "In four hours we will arrive in Omaha, Nebraska. We have to wait in Omaha only three hours, and that will be our last transfer before Portland, Oregon."

"How much longer do we have to travel to reach Portland?" Mother asked.

"Only forty-eight hours, Mother," I told her. "And I am sure Uncle George will be at the depot in Portland to meet us."

While crossing the Great Plains, I some-times saw cows out in what had been cornfields during the summer.

"Gleaning?" I asked myself, remembering my own gleaning in Germany the past four autumns. Only these cattle were gleaning corn fodder, not potatoes or sugar beets.

Seeing early November snow on the ground, I felt so sorry for the cows. I said to my brother, "Fritz, don't the farmers in the U.S.A. have barns for their cows?"

Fritz looked at me the way a big, knowl-edgeable, well-informed brother might look at his little sister. "Remember, Lilli, this is not Germany."

When, I asked myself, had this little brother of mine become my big brother? Al-ways in Germany he had been the boy of the family. Suddenly I realized that in America he was going to be the man of the family.

Farther west the large mountains amazed me. They looked as though they were made of sand instead of soil. Where were the grain fields?

In discussing this with Fritz, I got another grown-up answer from him. He said, "They probably can't use those mountains for grow-ing anything, but we can find out when we reach Portland."

Again I looked at Fritz. Standing, he mea-sured almost six feet. In years he was pushing toward nineteen.

As we neared Portland, we became more and more excited about greeting our relatives. We looked forward to thanking them personally for all they had done for us.

"Do you remember Uncle George?" I asked Fritz, thinking of the pictures we had received in Germany. "On the pictures he and Aunt Lisa are standing in front of a brick building, probably their home. It looked to me like they were rich. There must be some places in the U.S.A. where rich people live, even if they are poor in New Orleans."

Again I looked at my schedule, now frayed from much use during four days of traveling. Always afraid we would miss getting off at the right place, I had opened and closed that schedule again and again.

Finally we heard the conductor call out, "Next is Portland!" Nervous and excited, we grabbed our few belongings and stood, waiting for the train to stop. It still seemed hardly real that after all our years of suffering, planning, and praying we were in Portland at last.

As we stepped off the train and started walking toward the depot, I looked around for Uncle George. Thanks to the pictures, I recognized him, standing with another couple in front of the depot.

Greeting Uncle George was a touching experience. So was meeting Mr. and Mrs. Ganke, his friends who were sponsoring Ida. Their use of the German language both thrilled and relieved us. For four days we had spoken to no one outside of our family and the C.W.S. helpers at train stations. Now once again we could hold continued conversation with others in our mother tongue.

"All of us will go to my house for supper," Uncle George told us. "That includes the Gankes. My wife, Lisa, is planning for all of us as soon as we can get there."

Uncle George had our family ride with him in his car and the Gankes followed in theirs.

We gazed open-mouthed at things we saw along the streets and put question after question to Uncle George.

"Where is the man that changes the lights?" I asked, staring at the traffic lights as they turned red or amber or green.

"Those lights don't need people to operate them," Uncle George answered. "They are automatic."

That was astonishing to us. In Germany automobile traffic was so scant that automatic traffic lights had not yet been installed.

Electrically-lighted signs outside merchandise houses and grocery stores amazed us also.

Still staring and exclaiming at things we saw, we arrived at our uncle's home. Uncle George's mother greeted us warmly in German. How that pleased us! Uncle George's wife, Aunt Lisa, could not speak German. All she and I could do was put our arms around each other and smile.

We could hardly help looking around without showing curiosity. The house was new. In the next room were beautiful chairs and sofas. The large dinner table was set very artistically. A nice fireplace was built into the wall, and a brisk fire was burning.

That fireplace really attracted me. It drew my attention more than anything else. I had never seen a fireplace before. I could not understand why anyone in a nice home would want to have a fire burning. I kept watching and watching the fire, thinking it might be for cooking, though I could not see a cooking pot anywhere. Finally I got up enough courage to ask Uncle George, "Why do you have that fire burning?"

He said, "We have it just to be comfortable."

I thought, "Can looking at a fire be so comfortable?"

Supper was soon ready and we were called to the table. Mr. Ganke asked the blessing and we began to pass the food.

Our first supper in the United States! Never had we seen so much food for one meal, especially so many different vegetables, prepared in so many different ways.

"The squash in this custard is from our garden," Uncle George announced, passing the dessert. "I saved it especially for you, since we knew you would arrive some time in November."

What an evening that was! I am not able to express the gratefulness I felt toward them for all they had done for us the past four years. Now we could look into their faces and thank them personally. Now we were where we had been waiting and praying to be. It had paid us to be patient, to trust in the Lord for guidance, and to follow as He led.

It was hard to believe the evening had gone when the Gankes said, "We have to go home."

Ida knew she would go with the Gankes. They had sponsored her because they needed a girl to help with the housework. Uncle George had told Mother and Fritz to stay with them for several weeks until their neighbor's garage would be ready for them to rent. But what would happen to me? Where would I go?

The Gankes decided to take me along too, but said they could keep me only several days because they did not have an extra bedroom for me.

I thought, "I don't need a bedroom for myself. In Germany four of us lived for four years in one little bedroom, except that Fritz slept in the hall."

I kept those thoughts to myself, however.

The Gankes got ready to leave. Ida and I took our most needed things and said good-by to Mother and Fritz and our newly-found American relatives. I found it hard to leave Mother. I loved her and felt I needed to help her.

Ida and I traveled the five miles to the

Gankes' home in silence. I did not ask aloud the many questions struggling within me.

The Ganke home, like the Buchholz home, was beautiful. Now I could see that American people were rich.

The next morning Mr. Ganke went to work. Since Mrs. Ganke could not speak German and we girls could not speak English, the three of us did little more than look at each other all day.

Mr. Ganke came home from work with a big smile. He said to me in German, "Well, Lilli, my friend told me he has a job for you. After supper I am going to take you for an interview."

I prayed inwardly, "Jesus, please help me."

Much food graced the table, but I had very little appetite. I was thinking about my interview.

On the way Mr. Ganke began to explain to me. He said, "My friend is manager of a golf course club. They have a large building and they need a girl for cleaning."

I had no idea what a golf course was. He tried to explain to me. "It is a field where people have a stick in their hands and try to hit some small balls." It was no use to explain further. I could not get the idea anyway. A potato field would have sounded much better to me.

We arrived at the club house. Mr. Ganke's friend came to meet us in front of the building. Together we went in, Mr. Ganke telling me in German what his friend was saying. They showed me the rooms with all the large sofas and chairs. I felt afraid. It was such a large building and it was so dark inside. Then we came to what frightened me beyond words, the washrooms. I had never seen so many little stalls with sinks and showers. I nearly dropped to the floor when I was told my job would be to clean these washrooms on Saturdays, Sundays, and Mondays. They would put up a sign that would let anyone who came in know I could not speak English. In case a rich lady would like to have her shoes cleaned, the sign would help her know how to speak to me.

On the way back to Ganke's I said, "This is only three days. What will I do the other four days?"

"Oh, don't worry," he told me. "I will find other housework for you."

"But I don't have a place to live," I went on, trying to hide my tears. Besides, I thought, would it really be the Lord's will that I clean washrooms and ladies' shoes on Sundays?

Back at Ganke's Ida asked, "Did you get the job?"

I told her the situation. Not wanting to talk more, I excused myself and went to her bedroom. There I got down on my knees and poured out my heart to God. I knew He had the answer for me. Deep peace filled my soul; then I knew for sure the Lord had another job for me.

Several mornings later I got up quite early to talk to Mr. Ganke before he left for work. I asked him if he knew of any dairies that might need help.

"Oh, yes," he said. "There are quite a few dairies in this area. I know of one owned by Swiss people named Gruner. They probably can speak German. They are wonderful people."

"Mr. Ganke, I have worked hard all my life. I am willing to do practically anything, but I would not like to clean washrooms on Sunday. What would my Christian friends in Germany say if they heard about it?"

Mr. Ganke tried to put me at ease. "Don't worry. I will call the dairy today," he promised. Then he left for work.

I would have liked to help Mrs. Ganke with her housework. I watched everything she did, and soon I could help her a little without speaking. This was my fifth day with the Gankes. They had said I could stay with them only several days. Inwardly I prayed during the day, "Jesus, please do a miracle somehow. You know what is best for me. Don't let Mr. Ganke forget to call that dairy today. If You want me there, I am sure they will take me, and I hope at least one person among them can speak German."

I watched the clock. Soon Mr. Ganke would be home from work. I heard a car coming up the driveway. Yes, Mr. Ganke was home. I ran out to meet him.

"Lilli, I did not forget to call," he told me. "They sounded very nice on the phone, and told me to bring you to the dairy as soon as I came home from work. So if you will get your suitcase I will take you over right now."

"Praise the Lord," I almost shouted. "I am ready."

I grabbed my suitcase and jumped into the car. Was I really on my way to my job?

It took only a few minutes to get to the dairy. I received a warm welcome from the Gruners, and after a short conversation with them, I was hired. Then I knew I had a place to stay. I thanked God for answering my prayer. Now I would not have to clean washrooms on Sunday, and I would not need a sign saying I could not speak English. God had brought me to a home where the owners could speak German, and where they were very friendly. Their workers seemed to be included in the family, even calling Mr. and Mrs. Gruner Grandma and Grandpa. But best of all, the Gruners were a dear Christian family.

It pays to serve Jesus. What would I have done in this need without the Lord? To whom would I have turned? I have to say it again: it is wonderful to be led by the heavenly Father's hand.

I found myself in a completely new and different world. I had to learn many things all at once. I wanted so much to please everybody with whom I worked, yet I felt that at first I was more bother than help. No matter how hard I tried, what I did usually turned out not to be the American way. Still, the friendliness of the people made things easier for me.

After I learned some words in English, I began to use them. Sometimes I made very funny mistakes. Let me tell you about two.

In the morning when the men came to the kitchen for breakfast, each one would tell me what he wanted. When I took their filled plates to them at the table and they said "Thank you" to me, I said "Please" in return. To me that meant, "You are welcome." I noticed strange looks and grins on the men's faces, but I didn't know why. This went on for some time. Finally, one morning Grandma Gruner was in the kitchen and heard it. She looked at me and asked, "What did you say?" I said, "Please. Did I say it wrong?" She kindly told me, "You should have said, 'You are welcome,' instead of 'Please.'" Embarrassed, I then understood why the men had given me those strange looks.

Another time when Grandma Gruner was stirring up a cake, she told me to go to the cookhouse next door and bring her some marshmallows. I had never heard the word marshmallows before. I thought what Grandma wanted was marshmilk which in Germany is something like buttermilk. I ran to the cookhouse and said to the cook,

"Grandma would like to have some marshmilk." The poor cook studied every bottle in several refrigerators, but was unable to find any marshmilk. Finally he gave me a bottle of milk saying, "Give this to Grandma. I know this is good milk." Proudly I took it back to Grandma. I could see from the look in her eyes that I had made some mistake. Kindly she showed me a marshmallow. Then I learned that there is no such thing in America as marshmilk.

I was amazed at the friendliness of the people I found in America, and at the scanty attention paid to social levels. I could hardly believe what I saw when the Gruners, owners of a 125-cow dairy, ate at the same table with the men who were milking their cows or doing other jobs for them. In Germany such owners would usually eat in a different room. How privileged I felt to have come to a country like this! Also, in Germany cultures never mix. A person moving from one section of Germany to another would be respected in the new community but not accepted. I thought of Friedgard, whom I had known in West Germany, who was in love with a very fine man from East Germany. Her parents thought it a shame for their daughter to marry a refugee from the East, and they made her life very hard. Finally, unable to take the strain any longer, and seeing no way out, Friedgard had committed suicide. How happy I felt to be in a country where I was accepted and where the rich and the poor could eat at the same table!

Even though I found the going a little rough at times the first several weeks, I never became homesick for Germany. Being in a completely different world and unable to speak the language in that world could have discouraged me, but I found the way of living so much better that the language barrier grew small to me. Little by little I hoped to speak and act like the rest of the American people.

I enjoyed working at the Gruner dairy very much. Besides liking the work, I liked seeing and meeting the people who came there. Many school children visited the dairy. After their guided tour through the barns where they saw cows, ponies, sheep, goats, pigs and chickens, and where they were allowed to pet some of the animals, they were invited to the house where we served them ice cream and cookies.

My first experience in a restaurant was an unforgettable one. Several girls who worked with me at the dairy took me out for dinner. I had never seen such a place before. Many new things took my attention, but my biggest surprise came when I noticed waitresses carrying water to every person who came in, without even asking whether he wanted water. Puzzled, I thought, "Can every person really be thirsty at the same time?"

Quietly I sat down with my friends and waited, wondering what would happen next.

Soon the waitress set glasses of water before us. I was not thirsty. I had not asked for water. In a restaurant in Germany, if someone wants water, he has to ask for it. Here, I learned, it was customary to serve water to everyone, whether he wanted it or not.

When the girls asked me what I would like to order for my dinner, I was unable to tell them. What they ordered for me, however, was very good, and I appreciated their kindness in treating me to this restaurant dinner.

Nearly every day I faced something new and different. I always tried my best to react as Americans would, and to do things the American way. It was impossible to learn everything at once, however, and I often blundered. I appreciated the kindnesses shown me by the Gruner family. They had taken me into their home and had given me a place to live at a time when I needed help the most. They had shown me patience and understanding in my bewilderments over language, customs, culture, and behavior. I will always remember what they did for me. May God richly bless them for it.

Before long we found a spiritual church, began attending, and made many dear friends.

One Sunday afternoon we were asked to come to church. When we arrived, we were told there was a surprise for us—a welcome party—and we were called up front. There we were showered with beautifully wrapped packages that had been hidden away for us, and were told to open them. This was a new experience for us. We did not know what to say. Embarrassed, and feeling that we were objects of charity, we began to cry. Our hands shook as we tried to open those packages. When we finally got them open, we found beautiful gifts for our home. Later we were told by our friends that it is a custom in the United States to give welcome showers when new people come into the church from a different country. Then we felt better, and expressed unabashed gratitude for such thoughtful kindness.

Six months went by. I could speak English well enough to make myself understood. I could handle myself acceptably in American society. But I suffered over the separation of our family. Ida lived with her sponsors, the Gankes. Fritz and Mother lived in the garage that had been converted into a house for them. I stayed at Gruners.

Mother, in poor health, anxiously looked forward to having us all together again. Every Sunday, the day I (and Ida when she could) spent with her, she would ask, "Are you coming to live with us soon?" She was used to having me around, especially after we lost our papa. From that time on she had put much of the responsibility on me, even as a teenager.

I felt needed at home with Mother and Fritz. Ida wanted to be at home too, and she wished she could get a job that she could hold while living at home.

The idea of being together again as a family was exciting, but I felt guilty about leaving the dairy. I loved the Gruners and did not want to hurt them. Grandma was like a mother to me. But after I explained our situation, she understood.

Our family prayed and God wonderfully provided. Fritz, Ida, and I all found good jobs that allowed us to live at home with Mother.

God is always the same. In every situation He is worthy of our trust. He never leaves nor forsakes us when we trust Him with all our heart.

If you have a problem, turn to Jesus for help. What He has done for me, one of the least of His children, He can do for you. He is coming soon. What will you do if you are not ready to meet Him? "But who may abide the day of his coming? and who shall stand when he appeareth?" (Malachi 3:2). "It is a fearful thing to fall into the hands of the living God" (Hebrews 10:31). "He that overcometh shall inherit all things; and I will be his God, and he shall be my son" (Revelation 21:7). In America I found myself in a different world, but as my heavenly Father was with me through the war when the bullets were dropping around me, so He was with me here. Praise His name forever!

XIII

WHERE IS PAPA?

Now that all three of us children had found jobs and could all live at home with Mother, we needed a larger house. We discussed this and tried to plan. With our limited use of the English language, however, we found it difficult to inquire in the business world. Not knowing the laws in America, we did not know whether we needed permission from the city to find another place to live or not. In Germany no one could move freely.

When I finally asked Uncle George he explained, "All that you have to do here in America is to find a place you like, move, and pay your rent. You don't need to have permission from the city."

"What a wonderful country!" we thought. We loved it.

We began looking for a house to rent. It didn't take us long to find one since we felt that just anything was good enough for us.

The dear Gruner family sent a man with a truck to help us move. How we did appreciate that!

In Germany we had had one little room

which we had used for everything. Now we found ourselves in a three-bedroom house, hardly knowing what to do with all the rooms.

Finding ourselves in a wide-open, free world made us feel like birds let loose from their cage. We could hardly believe we could move around so freely. I did not need to find all those different offices to be registered, as I had had to do in Germany. I cannot explain what such freedom meant to us. So after seven years of living with others, all of a sudden, we had the liberty to live alone in a house and the joy of belonging once again.

Those were unforgettable, exciting days, spent largely in learning a completely new way of living. Our family took on American ways quickly. When we had friends for dinner or supper, for instance, I remembered my first experience in the restaurant and made sure I had water on the table, a glassful for every person, whether he was thirsty or not.

In a short time we made many dear friends. All the love we received meant much to us, because for years other people had had to take us into their homes. We had often felt we had not been wanted. Now we knew we were loved without obligation.

The Lord blessed us so richly that in less than two years we were able to buy ourselves a little home. Uncle George had some furniture he let us use until we could buy our own. People even gave us rugs for the floor and curtains for the windows.

"To me this seems like a miracle," Mother said.

"I shall never forget how rich I feel," I said as the tears and memories of our past wanderings flooded me again. "Is it true? Does it really belong to us?"

Our first meal in our new home was very special to us. Ida and I set the round table in the dining room. We put a beautiful tablecloth on it that we had received in the welcome shower at church. In the middle we placed a vase of flowers. Then we arranged plates, silverware, and other things, and finally the food.

Mother said grace on this first meal, just as she had done on our last meal in our home that we had to leave behind.

After we finished eating, Mother looked at us and asked, "Children, do you remember our last meal in our home when Hitler made us escape? Do you remember, how desperately we prayed, and put ourselves in the hands of God?"

"Yes, Mother, we do remember," we answered. Then for some time we sat around the table recalling God's goodness during our experiences as refugees.

My thoughts especially went back to that very special midnight hour when we were accepted in the Siegen camp. And I thought how much that experience has spiritual parallels. We had been mere travelers in West Germany with no home. So we are pilgrims and strangers in this world. We had longed for a home and had rejoiced when our names were finally written in the West German records. Similarly we long for our eternal home and rejoice that our names are written in heaven.

Is your name written in the book of life? Are you waiting for Jesus to come? Are you listening for His midnight cry? (Read Matthew 25:1-13.) Jesus may come very soon.

War had left marks on our family, marks that were difficult to erase. Often we relived the worst moments in our dreams and woke terrified, unable to go back to sleep. Sharing together and thanking God together was one way we were able to soften the scars and to replace the fears and heartache with peace and joy.

That evening our thoughts turned also to Papa.

Mother remarked, "It is comforting to know that he loved Jesus and loved to witness to others. I often wonder if he had a chance to be a blessing to someone who needed help."

"When Papa was with us," I said, "we usually had many friends coming to our home. We sang, played instruments, and talked of spiritual things. I loved that so much. Thankfully we again have friends coming to our home. We still sing and have fellowship, and the Lord amazingly blesses and comforts us. Still, our leader is missing."

One day I was marveling over the great

love of God. Then these words came to me which I put into a song. It was a great blessing to me. I just know it came from the Lord, so I would like to share it with you.

1) A gift of Love our God has given:
       He sent His only Son to earth
   To take our load of sin upon Him,
       and die alone, on Calvary.

2) The crown of thorns, his bleeding side,
       The bitter cup He took for me.
   It moves my heart when I remember
       He suffered there that I might live.

3) O let us work! The night is coming
       When man on earth can work no more,
   To tell the lost about the Saviour,
       And bring them in, into the fold.

4) Shall I receive a crown in glory,
       When I am entering heaven's gate?
   Or will there be someone to greet me,
       Whom I have led to Jesus here?

The house we purchased needed some remodeling. It had only two very small bedrooms, and we wanted to make the unfinished attic into a room for Fritz. But how should we go about finding a carpenter? I was still limited in my use of the English language, and I did not know any carpenter to consult.

Several weeks later an elderly man, Mr. David, came to us and said, "The Lord told me to come to you. Do you need any help?"

I looked at him in surprise. "Yes, Mr. David, we really do need help. We purchased this home, and now we need to have the attic finished. We were praying about it, asking the Lord to send us the right person. This is marvelous, Mr. David, that He has sent you to us. May I show you the attic?"

"Yes, I would love to see it."

We looked at the attic together, then returned to the living room to talk things over with the family.

After discussing plans and asking Mr. David to do the work for us, we waited for his answer.

He looked at me and asked, "Are you willing to buy the materials to finish the attic if I do the work free?"

Surprised, I answered, "Well, Mr. David, I would be more than happy to buy the materials, and I would love to pay you for your work also."

"Oh, no," he objected. "I will not take any pay from you for my work, because the Lord sent me to you to help you."

What could I possibly say? This was a direct answer to our prayer. Deeply moved, I smiled through my tears in gratefulness to God and to Mr. David who was listening to God's voice.

For weeks Mr. David worked on that remodeling, always insistent on bringing his own lunch and never taking any pay. And while doing all this, he often gave me much-needed advice on other things about the place. I was reminded of the Scripture, "Thou art the helper of the fatherless" (Psalm 10:14). God is true to His Word.

We attended church regularly. Ida and I were invited to join the choir. We could read English by now, and loved to sing.

In Germany, many churches, instead of having a choir, had groups of young people who sang, accompanied by guitars. Sometimes the people of our church asked Ida and me to sing as a duet. Not knowing the custom here in America, I played my guitar when we sang. One day I was told, "Here in America only cowboys play guitars." Embarrassed, I put my guitar away, and no longer brought it to church.

We talked often about Papa and Marie. If only we could hear from them! We had written the Red Cross in Germany, asking them for any information they might find about either one. This was all we could do, except pray, expecting God to answer according to His will.

Fourteen years went by. Then one day a letter came from the Red Cross in Germany.

"What will we find in it?" we wondered, almost afraid to open it.

"Have they found our papa?" was Mother's big question. "Or maybe they have learned that he died."

The letter gave us only the address of Marie

and her husband Rudi in Russia.

We wrote to Marie, asking her many questions. We especially asked whether she knew anything about our papa.

In a short time a letter came from Marie. With trembling hands Mother took it, saying, "Let me read it."

The tear-stained letter, written from Russia, told us that Marie and Rudi had accepted the Lord as their Saviour. Their new life in Christ was making all the hardship they had to endure much easier. Their adopted son had died. They knew nothing about Papa but were very happy to be able to write us.

The letter made us happy too. We had been praying for them for many years. Now we knew they were alive and that they were Christians.

Several years after we made contact with Marie, we received mail from other dear friends who had been transported to Siberia also. It meant much to us to keep in touch with them through letters and through prayer.

In one way our family does not like to talk about the tragic things we have gone through. Memories revive those frightening experiences. On the other hand, we like to talk about the many ways the Lord led us and protected us through all those dangers. We like to honor Jesus by telling what He has done for us so others can receive blessings also.

My purpose in writing this book is to testify for my Saviour. I have experienced over and over the wonder of trusting Him. When there was no human help available, I knew for sure I had Someone up in heaven watching over me. This Someone was my Heavenly Father, His Son Jesus, and His precious Holy Spirit—the great Three-in-One. This great God has created heaven and earth, yet He is mindful of little people like us.

In review, I wish to mention outstanding ways our God has been mindful of us.

In East Germany He had Uncle Gottlieb come and help us leave Lichtenburg. He provided a room for us with Aunt Frederika for a year until we crossed over the border into West Germany. In West Germany He had friendly Mr. Selzer furnish us a room in his house. In America He worked through Uncle George for the sponsoring of our family as immigrants to this country, where we now enjoy freedom and bounty. All these our family consider as miracles in our lives. We will never take them for granted. They were all direct answers to our prayers.

Jesus loves all of us very much. It is my desire and prayer that you who read this book, will also believe that we have a miracle-working God; and what God has done for us, He will do for you. But we must come to Him with all our burdens, whether they are great or small.

"Come unto me, all ye that labour and are

heavy laden, and I will give you rest. Take my yoke upon you, and learn of me; for I am meek and lowly in heart: and ye shall find rest unto your souls. For my yoke is easy, and my burden is light" (Matthew 11:28-30).

I wrote this as my testimony:
I can tell of His great mercy.
My friend, do you know who He is?
He is my Heavenly Father, His Son
Jesus became my Saviour,
And the Holy Spirit, my Comforter.
I do praise Him for His mercy.
Day by day He strengthened me
Even in the darkest hour.
Jesus never, never fails me.
    I do love Him for His mercy,
Because He first loved me.
With open arms He did accept me,
And forgave me all my sin.
When I reach that heavenly man-
    sion,
Which He prepared for you and me,
First of all I'll greet my Saviour,
Tell Him, praise Him, love Him.
Because He has redeemed a
Sinful soul like me.

After some years of living in America, our family has undergone changes, as may be expected. Ida married and moved to Canada. Fritz married and took up residence eight miles from us. Mother and I still live together.

I am rejoicing in the Lord. I count it a great privilege to belong to the family of God. It is my prayer and deep desire to tell others what the Lord has done for me.

Where is Papa? We are still asking that question. We have never heard what happened to him. We are almost sure that by now he is with Jesus, past all suffering, waiting for that great day when we all shall meet in heaven.

XIV

FROZEN POTATOES

Twenty wonderful years went by for me in America. I loved America. But as I kept receiving mail from dear friends who had been transported to Siberia, who had later returned, and who were now living in West Germany, I became more and more eager to see them again.

In trying to make plans for a trip to Germany, I learned about a Continental Club, Inc., that offered charter plane service to Frankfurt, Germany. Their flights were carefully planned with a leader or host who managed details for the passengers. By joining this club and waiting six months, I could get reduced rates.

I joined the club and was told I would be notified when a flight would be available. Then I wrote to my sister Marie in Russia, telling her about my planned trip to Germany.

In several weeks I received a letter from Marie, asking me to visit her friend Hulda in West Germany, whose address she enclosed. Marie and Hulda had lived in the same town in Russia until Hulda returned to join her husband in West Germany.

My scheduled flight would give me only a month in Germany. Would that allow me the time I would need to see the many friends I had there?

A dear lady friend told me about a Protestant convent in West Germany and suggested I invite my friends to meet me there. "I was there to visit my niece," she said, "and I know anyone is welcome, even without a reservation. You can stay as long as you like, and it is a beautiful place. I know you will enjoy it."

Following this lady's advice, I wrote to Hulda and to other German friends inviting them to meet me in that convent in West Germany.

Before long my flight organization notified me that there had been a cancellation of one reservation and that there would now be room for me on an earlier charter plane than I expected to get. Everything seemed to fall right into place for me, and I was very thankful. Happily I wrote my friends in Germany about my exact arrival time.

Full of expectancy and excitement, I boarded my plane for Germany. Soon I learned that nearly all of the 240 passengers spoke German. I then realized that my own German had become as poor as my broken English. Embarrassed, I tried my very best to improve my German.

At the Frankfurt airport, our flight organization had buses waiting to take us to the train depot. Riding the bus introduced me quickly to changes in Germany during the twenty years of my absence. Buses now had music playing in them. Some of the songs were the same as those I had heard in America.

Buying my train ticket to Eberstadt in the large Frankfurt train depot became an ordeal. Having never been to that depot before, I needed to ask for information, and I was surprised at the curt, short answer I received. I had forgotten that Germans are often not as friendly and helpful as the Americans. But I finally found my train to Eberstadt and then took a taxi to the convent.

A warm welcome awaited me at the Protestant convent. I happened to get there at the right time for the morning coffee hour which the Germans never miss. Guests from England and Chicago had arrived ahead of me, and all of us were invited to have coffee.

A sightseeing tour had been planned, and we guests were all invited to go along. We filled two buses which took us to some beautiful woods and mountains. On our way we sang some English choruses, making me feel as though I was back home in America.

Our tour guide told us that the convent sisters had claimed these woods and mountains by faith, and had prayed that God would someday let that whole area belong to the convent. God answered their prayers, and by a miracle the property came into their possession.

After we were shown some of the spots of special interest, we stopped in a beautiful place in the woods to enjoy the delicious lunch the sisters had prepared. We let the leisurely noon hour lengthen into afternoon, then climbed into our buses and returned to the convent. After a very good supper, we found comfortable rooms awaiting us, and we soon found ourselves in fluffy feather beds.

"Quite different from electric blankets in America," I told myself as I burrowed my way under the fluff.

Early the next morning I heard beautiful singing. On opening my door, I saw sisters walking along the hall singing hymns for all the guests in the building. Precious memories of that singing still come back to me.

Breakfast at 8:00 consisted of a menu different from what I was used to in America. Along with bread and sandwich meat, we had onions, tomatoes, and cucumbers.

After breakfast I began looking for the friends I had invited. All excited I walked back and forth in the entrance hall, wondering how many and who would come to see me. Would the sisters give them nice rooms?

The doorbell rang. The door opened and a lady walked in. She looked at me and I looked at her. Then I asked, "Are you Hulda?"

"Yes," she answered.

We put our arms around each other and began to cry. I felt almost as though she were my sister Marie. Then we went outside into the beautiful park and began to talk.

"Hulda," I said, "please tell me everything about Marie and Rudi. Do they have enough money for food? Do they have a good home to live in? Are they well?"

"Marie and Rudi are not very well," Hulda told me sadly. "They both have emphysema from working in the copper mines. They live in a two-room house. For food Rudi has to stand in line nearly every day. Those in authority have first choice. They take as much as they want. The other people get what is left over, but many times people have to go home without food."

Concerning herself, Hulda said, "When I returned from Russia, I brought only one daughter with me. My other six children are still there. We are waiting for their return. If only they could all see this beautiful place! Besides, I know how much they long to be with their father, now that he and I can be together again. My youngest son was one year old when we went to Russia. Now he is 27. He does not remember his father, who was taken into Hitler's army and then became a prisoner of the British army. After the British government released him, he returned to West Germany. Thanks to the Red Cross we found each other again. After 26 years I returned to join my husband. Now my husband can hardly wait to see all his children again. Our heart cry is, "Oh God, please bring us together again!"

After our walk we went to our room in the convent, which was offered to us as long as we wished to stay. Here we sat down, talked, cried, prayed, talked, and prayed again. Hulda was the first person I had met who had returned from Russia. I was so deeply moved and grieved by what she told me—things people in Siberia go through—that I thought I could hardly listen to more. Yet, I wanted to know all she had to tell.

"In the barracks where we had to live," she said, "we were very cold. We had no furniture. We slept on a little pile of straw on the floor. We didn't have enough blankets to keep us warm, and we had almost nothing to eat."

"You said you had seven children?" I asked.

"Yes."

"How old were they?"

"The oldest was 15 and very sick. The youngest was just one. I had to watch them suffer as they cried and begged for something to eat. They did not care what it was. Even a little potato soup made with water made them happy, just so they had something in their stomachs. Often I had nothing to give them. It was almost more than I could take. I prayed desperately, and the Lord heard my cry. Although daily I saw dead bodies carried out and people crying, all my children are alive today."

"What happened to those dead bodies?" I asked.

"A truck came and took them away."

"Where were they buried, and how?" I wanted to know.

"I only saw the trucks take the bodies away, but how and where they were buried I don't know. No one knows how many thousands have died in Siberia like that. Some years later conditions became a little better. We were moved by train to different towns or villages. Although we found better jobs, we were still very poor. Sometimes, however, we found stores where we could buy clothing or household articles, such as dishes, pots, and pans."

Hulda drew a deep breath and said, "This was my life in Siberia, full of hard work and suffering. Only those who have had the experience can really believe and understand."

Hulda had only twenty-four hours to spend with me before going home to her family. I felt very close to her, as though I had known her for many years. We promised to pray for each other, and said good-by.

None of the other friends I had invited to the convent could come. This was disappointing to me. But some wrote inviting me to visit them instead. They felt it would be easier for me to travel than for them since they had families.

Thanking the sisters for the good care they had given me during my stay at the convent, I said good-by to them. They promised to pray for me.

A two-hour train ride brought me to where my friend Marlene and her family lived. They also had returned from Russia. It brought me great joy to greet them. After a cup of coffee, Marlene began to tell me her life story.

"I was sent to Russia with my four children and my aged mother. There is a lot of work in Russia, and it seems they don't have enough workers. We were sent to a factory. The Russian government gave us ration cards, but we could not buy enough food with those cards to live on. We almost starved. Then my cards were stolen. In order to get new ones, we had to turn in some portion from our old ones. Having nothing to turn in, I could not get anything. At the government office, I wept and begged, 'Please have mercy; my family is starving to death.' The officer was not very concerned. He said, 'You should have known you are not living in Germany. Here people steal.'

"All my pleading with the officer did no good. I finally told him, 'I will not watch my family starve to death. If you do not help me soon, I am going to throw myself on the railroad tracks and let the train run over me. Then the government will have to take care of my family.' That softened the officer's heart, and he gave me more than I had lost. Oh, how thankful I was! From then on we did not have to fear we would starve to death."

"God has His own way of caring for His children," I thought as I listened to her story.

Marlene and I had a very good visit and a blessed time in prayer. We would have loved to have stayed in each other's company longer, but I had to leave and catch the train for my next stop.

As I neared the home of my long-ago neighbor, Anna, I got all excited. By the time I found her house number, my heart was pounding. I thought, "What will she look like after so many years of hard work and loneliness?" We had been close friends with her and her whole family, and this meeting with her was going to be very special.

I rang the doorbell. Anna came to the door.

"Anna!" I almost shouted as we fell into each other's arms.

"Come! Sit down and let's talk," she begged.

For several minutes we sat looking at each other without saying a word. She kept looking at my hands and finally said, "You don't have too many wrinkles in your face, but your hands look as though you have worked very hard."

"Yes, Anna, I did work hard, but I was not in Siberia as you were. I am sure you have worked much harder than I have in America. What was your job in Siberia?"

"I had to cut trees in the woods," she began. "The snow was so deep that we had to shovel it away before we could cut the trees down. It gets very cold in Siberia."

I listened with great compassion and had to

201

keep wiping tears. At what seemed like the right time, I asked, "Did you have food to eat?"

"Yes," she answered readily. "God was very good to me. A boy who had lost his family while Hitler was forcing people to escape came to live with me. Somehow he knew how to get food—how or where I don't know.

"Anna, where is the rest of your family?" I wanted to know.

"My sister, Lene, worked in the woods also but in another place. She became very ill. They took her to the hospital, and in several days she died. I learned about this through other people. How she was buried no one knew. Also through others I learned that my dear mother and father had died, but no one knew how they were buried or how they might have had to suffer before they died. They probably starved to death. When people became ill and could not work any more, they were not given any food."

I shook my head, almost unable to speak. "How could they get well if they had nothing to eat?"

"They couldn't," Anna said.

Our tears flowed. The heartache was almost more than we could bear. But then we shared how much the Lord had blessed us, and as we began praising Him, our burden became lighter.

Those few hours with Anna and her husband Fred were very precious to me. Fred had been in the German army and had become a prisoner of war in the American army. After his release he lived in West Germany until Anna returned from Russia. They were very happy to be together again after twenty-seven years of separation. In spite of all their suffering and loneliness through those years, they could say that God had been good to them.

Anna had found the Lord while in Siberia. That made me happy. And before I said good-by we joined in touching, compassionate prayer for each other.

Anna went with me to the train depot. When the train took me away, I stood by the window and waved to her as long as I could see her.

I was now on my way to the little village of Grosau, where our friend Susanna lived. Susanna had two daughters, Melita and Martha. Melita lived at home with her mother. Martha had worked in Hitler's army until the war ended. Then the Russian army had taken her as a prisoner to Siberia. We knew from our correspondence with Susanna after we came to America, that she had tried to get Martha out of Siberia. We knew too that Martha had married and was rearing a family. Now, as I neared Susanna's home, all these things came to my mind, and I thought, "How nice it would be if I would find Martha and her family back home in Germany with her mother."

As I looked through the window from my rolling train I saw we were passing by Grosau without stopping. A feeling of anxiety came over me when I found that the closest stop would be Hintersfelt. How far would that be from Grosau? How would I make my way to Grosau in the dark? How would I find Susanna's home?

I had learned at the first train depot that German conductors are not very friendly. I told myself not to ask too many questions.

Thankfully, on arriving at Hintersfelt and asking about the village Grosau, I was told it was five miles from the depot. My anxiety left me as a taxi took me right to Susanna's home.

Wondering who would come to the door, I rang the doorbell.

A lady opened the door. She looked at me. I looked at her. Neither of us spoke.

Moments later Susanna came, spilling out her welcome: "Lilli, it is you! How nice to see you! Don't you know who opened the door for you?"

"I am sorry," I faltered, "but I cannot recognize her."

"It is my daughter Martha!" she said.

Again I was speechless a moment before I could say, "Martha, is it really you?"

"Yes," she answered as we fell into each other's arms, "It is I."

While saying to myself, "You look like skin and bones," I said to her, "It is nice to find you here in Germany. When did you come home?"

"It is just one month today my family and I returned. Mother told me since I'm here you live in America. How do you like America?"

I smiled. "I do love America very much. I know there is not another country in the world that offers such freedom and abundance."

I had many questions in my mind to ask Martha about her life in Siberia. Should I ask them? Would I make her hurt all over again doing a review for me?

"Would you mind talking about your past life?" I finally ventured.

"Oh no," she answered. "I don't mind talking about it. Let's sit down."

We sat down while she continued, "You can ask me all you would like to know."

"First, Martha," I began, "how many children do you have, and where is your husband?"

She smiled enthusiastically. "I have two boys, and my husband works nights. You will meet him in the morning. One of my boys is four and the other is fifteen. The fifteen-year-old is in a boarding school, one hour by train from us. Germany has a free school for all who came from Russia. They can learn to read and write German. In Russia my son was in high school. Now here in Germany he is back in the first grade."

I saw tears rolling down Martha's face. I could feel the difficulty she was going through in adjusting. I tried to ease her by saying, "It is nice you can be with your mother. Since she is not well, I am sure she is very happy to have you here."

Sure that Martha had not finished with her story, I tried tactfully to bring her back to it as I said, "Now I would like to know about your life in Siberia."

Martha went on without hesitating. "We were like prisoners for several years. We did not have the choice of finding a better job or a better place to live. We lived with many people in a barracks."

"Did you work in the woods?" I asked, remembering Anna's account of cutting down trees.

"Yes, I had to load large logs on those big trucks."

"Martha!" I exclaimed. Could that be possible? "How were you able to get those big logs on trucks?"

"Oh, one girl went on the truck and pulled, and some girls from the ground pushed. It was easier to work with girls than with men, for men expected more strength from us girls than we really had. We had to load many logs a day. It was all piece work. They gave us one slice of very dark bread a day and some barley for soup, but not enough. The soup was so thin that we just drank it and went to bed. Our bed was a pile of straw on the floor. In the morning when we went to work, we carried the slice of bread in our pockets. If we didn't, it froze. It smelled so good as we walked to work that by the time we got to the woods and started to load, it was gone. We had to work hard and were so hungry. Many times we could not keep tears from rolling down our faces. We didn't know how it felt to have a full stomach. But God was with me. When the temperature was sixty degrees below zero and I was wearing regular shoes, He kept my feet from freezing. We girls had to watch each other so our faces didn't freeze. When we saw white spots on each other, then we had to rub our faces with snow. But I know my mother in Germany and many other Christians were praying for me, and for the others as well. We could feel those prayers. We would never have had the strength to do the hard work without them.

Moved with compassion, I thought, "How much suffering can a human being endure? And I have the privilege of living in America! How can I be thankful enough?"

We talked until late that night, sharing what God had done for all of us by lightening our burdens every day. Susanna, not being well, listened with great interest and with a thankful heart for answered prayer that her daughter could now be with her in Germany. Then we enjoyed a blessed time together in evening devotions. Melita read a scripture, and we had a time of prayer. It was a very moving experience to pray with these dear people who had come out of great suffering.

Conversation went on a while even after devotion. Martha especially could hardly stop. She said, "I know God protected my family in our hard life in Russia and arranged for us to come back to Germany. Still some things are difficult. We had to leave all our scant possessions in Russia. We were allowed to exchange only a little of our money and now we have to start all over again. Life is so different here in Germany. People cook and dress differently. In Russia life was very simple. I don't know if I will get accustomed to living here again."

"Oh, yes, Martha, " I told her. "Don't be discouraged. In a couple of months from now, you will feel altogether different. I remember that when our family started our new life in America, we seemed to be in a different world too. But we learned, and we loved it. Other people who have come out of Russia have told me they felt lost at first also."

"In one way even grocery shopping is hard," Martha said. "Shelves have so many different brands and varieties. People did not have that problem in Russia because the stores did not have so much."

Realizing that it had become very late, we finally had to say goodnight to each other and get to bed.

I could not sleep that night. My thoughts were with Martha and Susanna. I suffered with Susanna through the 26 years that she tried to get her daughter out of Russia. I suffered with Martha through her past month of trying to adjust to her new life. I could see how hard it was for both mother and daughter even now.

The next morning when I went to the dining room, I found Albert and Martha sitting there looking very sad.

"This is my husband Albert," Martha told me.

"I am so happy to meet you," I said pleasantly, and tried to begin a cheerful conversation with him. I soon noticed, however, that tears were rolling down his face.

"I had to leave all my brothers and sisters in Russia," he lamented. "Now I feel very lonely here. This village is so small, with only a little grocery store. My job is five miles from here, and there is no transportation."

"Please don't be discouraged," I begged both of them. "This is a free country. You can move to another town. You can find a better job. Things will go better for you in a few years from now. I've been told by many people who returned from Russia that the German government gave them thousands of marks. Even the money they had to pay for their passports in Russia was returned to them. You will receive aid too."

Martha and Albert listened very closely to what I said. Then Albert asked, "Do you mean everyone will get help from the German government?"

"Yes, Albert. All German people who come

out of Russia receive help."

Smiles came to their faces, and I had a good visit with them, though it was short. My time was so limited that I could stay only one day. As I said good-by, I wished them the Lord's blessing in their new life in Germany.

The Lord provided a way back to the train depot for me. He had a neighbor take me the five miles in his automobile.

As I waited in the depot for my train, I felt weary. I would soon be heading for my last visit in Germany before returning to America. My thoughts reviewed what I had learned from the people I had visited. Only in the strength of God had they been able to survive. It was precious to know that I could pray with them and hear from them how thankful they were in all their tragedies. Having gone through great heartache myself, I really could feel for them.

With new strength and courage, I boarded the train that would take me to Alice. I wondered what kind of story she would have to tell me. I had no desire to visit with fellow passengers on the train. Inwardly I kept praying that I might be a comfort and blessing to Alice.

I found Alice's home without difficulty. As we met, I marvelled that it was possible for us to be together. She and I had been in the same choir many years ago. Then she had gone to Russia and I, eventually, to America. Now, by the mercy of God, we could meet again.

"How do you like Germany, Alice?"

"To live in a free country like West Germany is wonderful. I can go to church, and I can feel real freedom," she answered, "but my heart aches for my daughter and her family. I had to leave them in Russia. Now my life is very lonely."

"Alice, where is your husband?" I asked.

That was almost too much for poor Alice to answer. If I would have known, I would not have asked.

"Lilli," Alice said, "my husband Otto was in the German army and became a prisoner of war in the British army, like many others of our friends. After his release he stayed in West Germany and built himself a beautiful home."

I noticed tears beginning to roll down Alice's face.

"Why don't you live with Otto?" I asked.

"He has a widow lady as a housekeeper. In Russia we had lived very simply. On arriving at my husband's I had to learn how to keep house in West Germany. Everything I did was wrong for him. Between the housekeeper and Otto they made life impossible for me. I cried day and night, and the loneliness for my daughter and family made my sorrow even greater." I stayed with Otto for only five months.

"What happened to your father?" I asked.

All she could say was, "We lost him through

war. Some people told me he was killed. My mother was transported with me to Siberia. She passed away after four years of suffering. That left me and my little daughter, five years old, in Siberia all alone."

"What kind of work did you do in Siberia?" I wondered.

"I had to carry water for the drill machines that exploded the stones for finding asbestos. In the beginning they were so mean to me. They made me carry two large buckets, which held about two normal-sized buckets each. In the winter time, the water froze on the outside of the buckets."

"Did you have enough to eat?" By now I had to keep wiping my tears.

"Lilli," she began with effort, "I worked nights carrying the water. In the daytime I walked miles to the train depot, went by train to a potato field to pick up frozen potatoes, and then walked all those miles home again. By the time I came home with my potatoes, it was time for me to go back to work."

"What did you do with the potatoes?" I both asked and exclaimed.

"I took the peelings off, salted them, and baked them on the top of the stove. We had no cooking oil. We were so thankful for those frozen potatoes. They kept us alive. Otherwise we would have starved to death."

Changing the subject from natural food to spiritual food, I asked, "Did you have a Bible or songbook?"

"I had a Bible, but no songbooks. When Hitler forced us to escape, we lost them and never found any to buy after that. I copied by hand over 300 songs which came through the mail from friends. We had no church, so we came together in homes for prayer."

While listening to her story, I had to think how merciful God had been to me. I was living in comfort in America. I told Alice, "My words are too few to express my gratefulness to God for His leading."

She answered, "Only through the strength that the Lord gave me was I able to endure."

I took Alice by the hand and we both dropped to our knees to praise God for everything—for the anguish and for the blessing—that had been ours.

This was Saturday night. After all the visiting and other excitement of the week, I felt worn out. I was happy to hear Alice say, "Can we go to bed now, so we will be rested for church by tomorrow?"

"Oh, yes, Alice, thank you," I told her.

Tired as I was that night, I lay awake for a long time, thinking about the hard life Alice had gone through. My heart ached at the thought of frozen potatoes. Frozen potatoes to keep her alive! Now here in West Germany where she should have had it easier, her husband would show her no mercy. Will there be a better day coming for Alice? How much more can she bear?

I remembered seeing people in America

throw away a lot of good food. I began to pray, "O Lord, give us Americans a burden for poor people who are in need. Make us understand what it means to suffer hunger."

When I awoke the next morning, I could hear Alice praying. After she finished, she shared with me what was on her heart.

"I have a great burden for my daughter and her family. If only they could return and live here!"

Soon it was time for church. I was very eager to listen to a good sermon, for I missed my church in America.

"How many services do you have on Sundays?" I asked Alice. "My church, and nearly all churches in America, have two services."

"We have only one," she told me.

The pastor preached a satisfying sermon that Sunday morning, and my longing for a good church was fulfilled.

After dismissal I said to Alice, "I wish we could stay here in church for a while. We could sing and fellowship with each other."

The pastor allowed us to stay, and we had a wonderful time together. It seemed to me as though we were carried back in time to our youth group again. Singing and talking there in the church, we suddenly realized it was time to go home.

That afternoon we were enjoying a cup of tea together when we heard footsteps, and then the doorbell rang. Alice went to open the door. What a surprise! Johana and Willi, friends of Alice! I had not seen them for many years.

"Sit down and make yourselves at home," Alice invited.

We all had some tea, and a good time of fellowship.

Then Johana suggested, "Could we go and visit Otto? I know he is not well. Maybe we can be a help to him."

I was happy to hear that. I had known Otto even before the war, and I felt I really would like to see him before I went back to America.

"Does he live very far from here?" I asked.

"Oh, no," Alice said.

"We all can go in our car," Johana offered.

"That would be fine. I can show you the way," Alice said. "Willi and I will wait in the car for you, while you visit with Otto. I am sure he will be happy to see both of you."

On our way to Otto, I kept wondering, whether he would remember me. Would he be friendly?

I rang the doorbell. Johana stood behind me. Slowly the door opened, and Otto faced us.

"Do you remember me?" I asked.

He looked at me for a minute, then said, "No, I do not."

Johana spoke up. "Don't you remember me either?"

"Oh, yes, I do remember you now."

"This is Lilli," Johana introduced.

He invited us into the house. After a short

visit he showed us around the house. At the back door, there was a small room with a chaise lounge in it. He pointed to this, saying, "There Alice used to sleep."

My heart felt broken. I had to hold back my tears, saying to myself, "How could he treat her so mercilessly, after all she had gone through in Russia rearing their child by herself and eating frozen potatoes to stay alive? And he had been in comfort in West Germany most of those years!"

When we were ready to leave the house, I asked Otto, "Do you have a Bible?"

He answered, "Yes, there must be one in the basement."

After a short silence, I said to him, "Otto, there is coming a day in your life when you will need help from God very desperately. God loves you. He sent Jesus to die on the cross for you. It is so simple. All you have to do is believe. Where will you turn if you reject the Bible?"

He smirked. "Who reads the Bible in our modern days?"

There was nothing more we could do for him. Sadly Johana and I said good-by to him and went our way.

We all stepped into the car and were on our way again back to Alice's home. We had seen Otto. We also had told him of his spiritual need, but we could not change him. The Holy Spirit would have to do what we could not do.

Before Johana and Willi left for their home,

we joined in prayer for Otto and for all the rest of us. Then they said good-by.

Now Alice and I had only a few hours left to spend together. Moved with deep compassion, I looked at her, but I could not at first find words to comfort her. She was so very broken. Then several Scriptures came to me. "In all thy ways acknowledge him, and he shall direct thy paths" (Proverbs 3:6); and, "But Jesus beheld them, and said unto them, With men this is impossible; but with God all things are possible" (Matthew 19:26).

"Have faith, dear Alice, and look to your Heavenly Father," I told her. "He has brought you through much hardship in your life thus far. I am sure He is with you here in West Germany also. I believe the day will come when Otto will ask you to come back to live with him. Alice, in all our suffering and sorrow, what would we have done without Jesus? Just think, He loved us so much that He gave His life for us so that through Him we can have everlasting life. Let's rejoice that Jesus is coming very soon. Then we can live with Him forever. The Bible says, 'But as it is written, Eye hath not seen, nor ear heard, neither have entered into the heart of man, the things which God hath prepared for them that love him' " (I Corinthians 2:9).

We both praised the Lord; and new strength, peace, and joy filled our hearts.

I looked at the clock and exclaimed, "Alice! In one hour I must be at the train depot!"

"I will go with you to the depot," she offered.

Together we walked, holding to each other as tightly as possible.

Our last minutes together passed quickly. As my train came rushing in, we had to tear ourselves apart. I said, "May the Lord bless you, and good-by, Alice. Stay near to the cross, and Jesus will stay near to you."

My heart both sang and cried as I settled into my seat on the train. For almost a month I had been rejoicing and weeping with friends who had returned from Russia. I had listened to their triumphs. I had listened especially for word about my papa. Had any of them seen him? Was he in good health? Would he return someday also? Nobody had any information, and I had to leave Germany still wondering.

As the plane lifted into the air and soared over the Atlantic toward America, I thanked God for the blessed hours I had spent with my friends. What inspiration I had received from their simple gratitude to God for keeping them through the nightmare of war and for providing strength for them to do their hard labor without enough food or good clothing. I knew I would never forget Alice's thankfulness for frozen potatoes.

The whole way across the ocean, memories of what I had seen and heard stayed with me. And as my plane descended for Seattle, I asked myself, "Am I really thankful enough for everything I have here in America?"

XV

BORN AGAIN AND RETURNED

Shortly before Christmas in 1973, a note came from my sister Marie and her husband Rudi, mailed in West Germany.

"Mother!" I exclaimed as I began reading. "They have returned from Russia and are living in West Germany now. After being ill for fifteen years and hardly able to walk even to the grocery store for needed food, they must be greatly relieved to be in Germany. This is nothing less than a miracle."

Mother rejoiced with me.

"I'm so excited," I bubbled. "I think I'll go to visit them. I haven't seen them for nearly thirty years, you know."

Almost before I knew it, I had plane reservations made and a letter off to Marie telling her my schedule. And two days after Christmas I found myself fastening my seat belt, airborne for Frankfurt, Germany.

On my way I began wondering what to expect at my coming meeting with Marie and Rudi. How ill were they? Would they be able to meet me at the train depot? Would the excitement be too much for them? They had written us very little about their health or personal welfare. I had learned some things through Hulda, who had met me at the Protestant convent in 1971. Hulda had lived in the the same town with them before her return to West Germany. What I knew gave me some concern about the effect my arrival might have on them.

Many friends in America knew about my trip and had promised to pray that the Lord would work things out for all of us. This gave me great comfort and confidence.

After landing in Frankfurt, I took the train to the town where Marie and Rudi lived, expecting to see them at the depot waiting for me. Not finding them there, I took a taxi to their home.

On entering and seeing them, I stood speechless a moment, shocked. How difficult their breathing sounded! But I dared not tell them so. How wasted and aged they looked! What could I say? How should I start?

"Praise the Lord!" I cried, falling into their arms. This broke the tension, and we laughed and wept at the same time. I shall never forget the sacredness of that meeting, and the prayer of thankfulness we prayed with joined hands. How we praised God for letting us see each other again after thirty years of separation! I had never been able to pray with Marie and Rudi. I had never known them as Christians. Now God in His mercy fulfilled my longing to fellowship with them in the Lord.

Praise His wonderful name forever!

Marie and Rudi had planned to meet me at the train depot, but somehow in the turmoil of adjusting to a new life in Germany, they had confused the dates. This was very understandable and easy to overlook.

"We have been praying that God would help us not get too excited," Rudi said. "That would be bad for Marie's heart."

"I have been praying too," I said.

"Surely, God answered our prayer and I did not get excited," Marie said. "It was all planned by God."

A quick glance around the room made me guess that these four walls enclosed all of what Marie and Rudi had to call home. Cookstove, table, chairs, and bed showed plainly this room served as kitchen, living room, and bedroom, all in one. I learned later they shared a small, poorly equipped bathroom with another family who lived in another room.

Marie noticed me looking around the room.

"We are not planning to live here very long," she explained. "The government is building apartments for us. When they are ready, we will move and have a nice place to live."

I began unpacking things I had brought for them—a big bowl of Christmas cookies, some dried apples and prunes Mother had prepared, a teapot, sweaters I had made from woolen materials, and other pieces of clothing. Knowing that Marie and Rudi had just set up housekeeping, and that they likely had very little of anything, I tried to bring things they would need most. The many exclamations of gratitude, along with the wiping of tears, told me I had supplied some of their most urgent needs.

My turn to wipe tears came next. Marie went to her clothes closet, took out something wrapped in a cloth, unwrapped it, and held it out to me, saying, "Lilli, I give you this gold wristwatch."

Drawing back, I asked, "Do you have one for yourself?"

"No. I was allowed to bring only one out of Russia."

"But, Marie," I objected, "I cannot take it away from you if you don't have one."

"Lilli," she insisted, "I would like to give it to you in appreciation for all you did for us in sending those parcels of clothing when we were still in Russia. Your thoughtfulness meant so much to us."

Rudi spoke up. "We also received the Bible you sent."

"Oh," I said with joy, "did you really receive it? Praise the Lord!"

"Yes, it was a beautiful little Bible. And we received the songbook as well. Both are highly treasured in Russia."

Marie added, "And we received that Bible on a very special day—on Good Friday. I was so happy. I took that Bible and pressed it to my heart and marched up and down my room thanking God for it. On Good Friday Jesus was crucified. He willingly died for every person in the world. Now I had a Bible where I could read about the love of God and His only Son who was willing to die."

Tears rolled down Marie's face as she added, "Very few people receive Bibles in Russia. I was so thankful that people in other countries loved us and cared for us enough that we could have the Word of God also. And, Lilli, I want you to have this wristwatch."

I took the watch with deep gratefulness, unable to express my feeling. She was giving me the most priceless thing she owned, and it was difficult for me to accept. I put my arms around her and said with deep feeling and many tears, "Thank you, Marie," while asking myself, "Would I be willing to give someone the best, most-prized thing I own?"

I could not help noticing Marie's deeply wrinkled face, her stooped back, her yellow face, her blue lips, and her heavy breathing. Her pathetic condition nearly broke my heart.

Together she and Rudi began telling me their tragic story.

"Rudi had to go to the German army," Marie said. "Then a few months later our family was forced by Hitler to leave by horse and wagon. The Government furnished the transportation."

"Did you suffer much while you were on the road?" I asked, remembering our own escape.

"Oh, yes," she answered. "It was terrible. We had to travel day and night. Our only food was bread and jam which we had brought from home. Sometimes we found a place where we could make something hot to drink. Otherwise we lived on the bread and jam."

"Did you see a lot of shooting as you went?" I asked again.

"Oh, yes. It was so frightening. The roads were narrow and were packed with refugees. No one could turn around and go another way, as the roads had deep ditches on each side. When the soldiers with their war tanks came in, there was not enough room for them to pass our caravans of wagons. We had to jump off our wagons and into the deep snow to keep from being run over. Sometimes there was so much shooting going on between the Germans and their enemies that we even lay down in the snow. We could hear the bullets flying around us; but, thank God, our family was not hurt.

On one occasion when the shooting was over and all the soldiers were gone, we crawled out of the ditch and looked for our wagon. The tanks had run over it. We had lost everything except a little clothing and some bedding. Now, with horses and wagon gone, there was nothing for us to do but walk. For days we tried to find a place to live. We knew we could not return to our home, for it had been destroyed.

"Rudi's elderly mother and father were with us. Walking was terribly hard for them in the deep snow and cold weather. It was hard for my fourteen-year-old son also. I guess it was hard on all of us.

"One day as we were walking along, my father-in-law said, 'I am all exhausted. I am not going to walk any more.' What could we do? We could not carry him, and there was no transportation available. Although we begged him to come with us, he kept saying, 'I can't walk any more,' and he sat down in the snow on the road. Then I did something that embarrassed me terribly. I couldn't understand why I did it. He was carrying a little bag of sugar which he had tied in the buttonhole of his coat. In my frustration as I stood there in front of him, I untied that little bag of sugar and threw it as far as I could into the snow. Then all of us begged him again to walk with us. After a while he turned to me and said, 'Marie, if you bring back my sugar bag, I will walk again.'"

"What a time I had looking for that little bag in the deep snow! I cried bitter tears, but I did not know how to pray. Finally I found it. I felt as though I had found a piece of gold. Father kept his word, and we went on.

"Eventually, we found a place to live. But there were no jobs to find anywhere. Because Russia had too much work and not enough people, all of our family, along with thousands of other German refugees, were transported to Russia.

"In Siberia we were housed in barracks, which were very cold. We were given very little wood or coal for heat. The food that was given to us was not nearly enough to live on. We were afraid we would starve to death. In desperation we, along with other German people, took some of our belongings, mostly clothing, and walked to the Russian villages. There we went from house to house trying to exchange it for a little something to eat. We needed the clothing badly, but by exchanging it for food, we were kept from starving.

"My assignment was working in the copper mine. Shortly after we were settled, our son became very ill, and in a few days he died."

"Did he love the Lord?" I asked. "Did he know how to pray?"

"Oh, no," Marie answered sadly. "He did not know how to pray. Neither did I at that time. He had mentioned to me quite often that it would be better to be dead than to live with our conditions.

"I had to dig the grave for my son," Marie went on. "It was terribly hard. Some others helped me to carry the casket to the cemetery. After that, three of us ladies talked it over and decided that when someone in our families passed away, we would help each other to prepare the grave.

"One year later my father-in-law passed

away, and we three ladies dug the grave. That made it a lot easier. It was winter, and in Siberia winters are extremely cold. We had no idea where to find transportation for bringing the casket to the cemetery. Someone told me there was a man living in the area who had a camel and some kind of wagon. I had no address, but I began walking and asking different people whether they knew where the man with the camel lived. After many hours of walking through deep snow, I found him. We were thankful that he was willing to come with his camel and sled. When we arrived at the cemetery and were about to lower the casket into the ground, we found that the grave was full of snow and also that it was not long enough. We ladies began to dig again in the ice and snow until the casket would fit into the grave."

"Did you have a minister?" I asked.

Marie shook her head. "Oh, no. We simply said the Lord's Prayer and sang a song. That was all we could do."

"I had been in the German army," Rudi said, "and had become a prisoner of war under the Russian army. Among thousands of other German soldiers, I was transported to Siberia and put to work in a copper mine also, though it was far from the mine where Marie worked. We did not hear from each other for three years. Then somehow through letters we found each other again and were permitted to move together. We still had to work in the copper mine until we became so sick we were unable to continue. The dust in the mines gave us emphysema, and our breathing became difficult. Then the government gave us a little pension and we bought a small, two-room house."

After visiting for several hours, Marie asked, "Could we have a cup of tea together?"

"That would be just great," Rudi approved. "I love tea."

We postponed further sharing to prepare the table for tea. I arranged the tablecloth and the bowl of cookies. We got the teapot ready with that good, American Lipton tea. Then we three gathered around the table for the first time in thirty years. I never can express my feeling of gratitude to God.

Deeply moved, I looked at Rudi and Marie. For years we had been praying that they would find Jesus as their Saviour and that God would give them strength and restore their health. God had answered our prayers. They were born again and returned.

I was reminded of the story in Acts 12:7-17 where Peter was brought out from prison by an angel. When he came to the house of Mary, the mother of John, where many were gathered together praying, they could not believe it was Peter—they thought it was his angel.

Before we had our tea, Rudi took the Bible and read Psalm 145:1-3: "I will extol thee, my God, O king; and I will bless thy name for ever and ever. Every day will I bless thee; and I will praise thy name for ever and ever. Great is the Lord, and greatly to be praised; and his greatness is unsearchable."

Rudi, now a minister of the Gospel, said, "Can we join the Psalmist David with our praise?" We all agreed. With tears of joy, we all praised God for what He had done for all of us. The presence of God was very near to us. To me it was a little foretaste of heaven.

After our relaxing tea hour, we began talking again.

"Now will you tell us some of your war experiences, Lilli?" Marie asked me.

"I will try," I told her. I told them the story of our hardships and the Lord's deliverance, lingering especially over the farewell with Papa. I told Rudi and Marie that as Mama handed Papa that last cup of tea, he had said he would rather spend his last few minutes with his family in prayer.

"So Marie and Rudi, you were included in Papa's prayers. As I listened to you just now, I know the Lord has answered Papa's prayers, keeping all of us alive through the dangers of war and hardship.

"Many times afterwards I saw Papa in a dream. He was home, and I tried to tell him our tragic experiences. Then I would ask, 'Papa, this time are you really going to stay with us?' I would try hard not to wake up for fear it might be just another dream. But I always woke up to find no one there to take my load. I had to keep carrying on. I would pray for new strength, bury my face in the pillow, and cry myself to sleep.

"Marie and Rudi, do you remember Uncle Gottlieb and his family?" I asked.

Marie answered, "Oh, yes we do. We lived with them a couple of months on his farm, staying on after Rudi left for the army. When they were forced to escape, we rushed home to Rudi's parents, so we could be together with them. We were very thankful to get home on time. We could have been separated. Many as old as they had to escape alone, and they died of starvation."

Then I told them how Uncle Gottlieb had helped us.

As we continued sharing, Marie looked at me and asked, "Where can we find an answer for all the suffering that war has caused?"

Rudi shook his head. "We cannot find an answer here. When we get to heaven we will understand it all. I could have been killed in the war. Many times I barely escaped death. But God always had His angel protecting me. How merciful He was! I didn't even know Jesus as my Saviour at that time."

"Can you tell me how you both came to be saved?" I asked.

"Surely," Marie answered. "While we worked in the copper mines, we were supposed to wear masks to keep the dust from getting into our lungs. But we could hardly breathe through them, and every couple of minutes we had to shake the dust out. That took so much of our time we did not put out enough stone to please our manager. The food we received was very little, and if we didn't put out enough stone, our food rations were cut still lower.

"My job was to pick up the stones and put them into baskets after they were broken up by a drill machine. Every basket was counted, and I was paid for the number of baskets I picked up. One day we noticed an immense piece of rock overhead that seemed to be just hanging. On every side of it, the rock had been chipped away. We knew it might fall any minute, and we were warned to be careful, but none of us could do anything about it. All of a sudden I heard workers scream, 'The stone! The stone!' I was working nearest the place where it came down. The tremendous pressure threw me out of the way as the stone landed on the ground, and only my knee was injured."

I interrupted, "I am sure it was not the pressure that saved your life, Marie. It was the hand of the Lord."

Marie agreed, then she continued, "Sirens began to blow. The manager blamed me for getting hurt because I hadn't watched the stone more carefully, and I was rushed to a hospital. Lying on my bed, I thought. 'What a miracle that I am still alive! If I had not been thrown out of the way, there would have been nothing left of me. There must be a reason.'

Then my mind went back to our childhood home. It seemed I could still hear Papa preaching and praying for all of his children. I remembered he had taught us that to make heaven our home, we needed to ask Jesus to forgive our sins. I had never asked Jesus to come into my heart. I had never prayed. 'Oh, my God,' I said, 'now I can clearly see the reason why my life was spared. I was not prepared for heaven.' Then I started to cry, and from my innermost self I prayed, 'Jesus, here I am. Forgive me all my sins. Take my life. I put myself into Your hands.

"After I prayed I could feel a wonderful peace flooding my soul. I had never known such peace. My burdens became lighter. I was a child of God. I was ready for heaven.

"After three months my knee was healed, and I was released from the hospital.

"Rudi saw the change in my life, and he began asking me questions. When he heard me pray, he asked, 'Did somebody teach you how to pray while you were in the hospital?"

I said, 'Oh, no. No one taught me how to pray. While I was lying in the hospital bed wondering in amazement why my life had been spared, I remembered how many times Papa had spoken to me about asking Jesus to come into my heart. Rudi, I could have been killed, and I was not ready for heaven. I was frightened and I cried out to Jesus, asking Him to forgive my sins. He did forgive me, and I am so happy now. Rudi, I feel so wonderful now. Jesus filled my heart with joy."

"Then Rudi asked me if he could be saved also. I was so happy! I prayed, and then Rudi prayed for the first time in his life. Great joy came into our home that day. Now we could go hand in hand for the rest of our pilgrim journey, with Jesus leading us.

"As we studied the Bible together, it became very clear to us that we needed to be baptized with water. Jesus said, 'He that believeth and is baptized shall be saved; but he that believeth not shall be damned' (Mark 16:16). We certainly did believe, and we wanted to be baptized."

"It was our desire," Rudi said, "that Marie and I might walk day by day in obedience to God the rest of our lives.

"When we went to the minister, he said four other believers wanted to be baptized also. He invited us to join this group.

"We came together that night in a home and prayed, first of all, for protection from harm. God answered by giving us great joy and courage. We felt surrounded by angels. It was almost midnight when we began walking toward the river. The moon was shining beautifully, and it was winter."

I stopped Rudi long enough to ask, "Do you really mean you were baptized in the river in the winter time?"

He answered, "Yes. The water was not frozen, but there was a lot of snow that we had to shovel away before we could go into the river.

We changed our clothes quickly right there by the river."

Again I had a question. "Did you have to walk very far to your home afterward?"

"Only three miles."

"Three miles!" I exclaimed. "Didn't you get sick?"

"Oh, no, we rejoiced in the Lord. It did not bother us at all."

I rejoiced also as I listened to this thrilling account. Marie and Rudi had shown true love for Jesus and real courage in Him. They had risked their very lives in obedience to Him. And they could say with Paul, "Nay, in all these things we are more than conquerors through him that loved us" (Romans 8:37).

A number of happy experiences came to me during my month with Marie and Rudi. Among these were meeting and visiting with old friends whom I had known from childhood, or had met after I had become a Christian. There were surprise visits and planned visits, and I thanked God for every one.

On arriving in Germany, I had written to Erna and Erich, former neighbors of ours in East Germany, telling them of my plans to spend a month with Marie and Rudi, and suggesting they should try to meet me there.

One day I received a letter from Erna telling me that her husband Erich was not able to travel and inviting us to come to her home instead.

"Do you know Erna?" I asked Marie. "She

and her three children lived next door to us in East Germany. They were a dear Christian family. They were sent to Russia to work. Her husband Erich was in the German army. Fortunately he became a prisoner of the British army, and after his release he lived in West Germany. After 27 years Erna returned from Russia to join him, but her three children were still there. Poor Erna was torn between the joy of reunion with her husband and the sorrow over the separation from her children. Four years later one son returned to them."

"No," Marie said, "I don't seem to know Erna."

I gave more of the family background. Suddenly Marie said, "Do you mean Adolfience Schulte is Erna's sister?"

I nodded.

"Oh, Lilli," Marie said, "Adolfience and her husband Gustaf came to visit us many times in Russia."

All three of us then decided to visit Erna and Erich, and we sent word that we would come the following weekend.

We received a very warm welcome, and we enjoyed rich fellowship in that home.

"We had two miracles in our home during the last month," Erna told me in the kitchen while we prepared the evening meal.

"Wonderful!" I beamed. "Please tell me about them."

"My husband Erich had a bad heart attack. He almost died. I prayed, 'Oh, my God, please, please don't take him. He is not ready to die. I've never heard him pray. He's never said he loves Jesus. How will he be able to stand before the judgment seat of Christ?' Praise God, Erich saw his condition and realized that there was no other help than turning to God. He started to pray and kept on praying and crying day and night until the Lord in His mercy saved his soul, and healed his body."

"Praise the Lord!" I almost shouted.

In the course of our visit with Erna, I asked, "Is Alice coming?"

Erna shook her head sadly. "Oh, no. Didn't you know her husband is very ill?

I interrupted. "Is Alice back with her husband?"

"Yes," Erna replied. "Here is a letter for you from Alice."

I had known Alice as a girl back home. So had Erna. Alice and Erna had kept up their friendship, and after marriage their husbands had become good friends also. Knowing all this, I had written to Alice and invited her to come to Erna's while I would be there, so we could all be together. Now as I read Alice's answer to my letter, it became clear to me that I should go to see Alice before returning to America. Perhaps I could talk to her husband about Jesus.

"I have my cassette tape recorder with me," I told the others. "Why don't we record some singing and testifying to play for Alice and Otto tomorrow?"

We all sang several songs. Rudi read a scripture and preached a short sermon. Then we all knelt for prayer. How Erich's prayer touched me! He overflowed with praise to God for saving his soul and healing his body. Erna, too, filled her prayer mostly with praise for bringing her to her husband again and for keeping her through the hard times in Siberia. She prayed also for her children still in Russia. All of us remembered to pray for Otto, that he would open himself to God for the same miracles Erich had just experienced.

That little prayer meeting was to me like a foretaste of heaven. The room seemed to be filled with angels, and I felt the presence of God.

Since Erich was a good friend of Otto, he gave his own testimony on the tape recorder, telling what the Lord meant to him and also pleading with Otto to follow Christ.

The hour grew very late. We had so much to share. This is something that can never be understood outside of Christ. When Christians meet for the first time, there is a feeling of having known each other all their lives. The bond of love is sweet. They are one great family of God.

The next morning after a good breakfast, Rudi, Marie, and I got ready for our little trip to Alice and Otto's. It was hard for the five of us to say good-by to each other. We all joined hands and prayed. Then we three departed with joy and peace in our hearts and tearful smiles on our faces, our last words being, "Praise the Lord."

The trip took several hours and gave me great concern for Marie and Rudi, for we had to change trains and streetcars, and the weather was cold and rainy. But Rudi and Marie met the rigors of the way bravely, wanting to learn how to travel around in Germany.

Unable to get word to Alice after receiving her invitation, we took her by surprise. She was very happy to see us, and gave us a warm welcome. Words came thick and fast in our exchange of greetings with her. We greeted Otto too, but we saw immediately that he was indeed very ill.

After visiting with them awhile, I asked Otto, "May we sing and pray?"

He answered with an expressionless "Yes."

Alice looked at him in happy surprise. He had never allowed her to talk to him about Jesus. When she had tried he had become very angry with her.

We gathered in the living room. Otto joined us. He even joined in the singing. Rudi read Scripture and explained the plan of salvation as clearly as possible. Then I played the tape we had made at Erna and Erich's home. Otto listened to the testimony of his friend Erich, hearing Erich say that what God had done for him, He could also do for Otto. Then we joined in prayer.

Otto knew he would not live long unless God performed a miracle. Yet he made no response. He seemed to feel no need of a Saviour.

"I have only one wish," Otto said, with tears rolling down his face, "that I could see my daughter and her family before my death."

Again, as on the night before, with so much to talk about, the hour grew late. All of us became very weary, especially Marie. Alice prepared a place for us to rest for the night.

Weary as I was, I felt I could not go to bed. I knew that Alice carried a heavy burden. My heart ached for her, and I wanted to comfort her. I took her by the hand and said, "Let us go and sit down and talk." Alice began to cry and then told me her story.

"When word came to me that Otto was alone and in the hospital, I felt led to go see him. His condition nearly broke my heart. I put my arms around him. I asked him if he remembered our marriage vows—how we had promised to help one another through sickness and health until death parted us. I told him I loved him and felt responsible to help him, and I asked him if he would let me come and take care of him in his home. Otherwise he would have had to go to a rest home.

"For a short time he was silent, and then he answered, 'Yes, you may come.'

"I am so happy I can be with him and help him in this last serious illness. It is hard for me to see him suffer. My prayer is that he will find Jesus as his Saviour and that our daughter and family will return very soon."

I said, "Alice, when you get to heaven, you will receive your reward for your kindness."

We finally went to bed, but I could not sleep. After a while I said to Marie and Rudi, "It is already midnight, but could we pray again for this home? I know God can perform a miracle."

After we prayed I felt a wonderful peace, and I thought, "Thanks be to God, which giveth us the victory through our Lord Jesus Christ (I Corinthians 15:57).

The next day I prayed inwardly for an opportunity to witness to Otto one more time before we would have to leave. I felt sure I would never see him again. God heard my prayer and gave me several minutes with Otto. I said to him. "Otto, what will you do when you stand before God? If you don't accept Jesus as your Saviour now, it will be forever too late."

Otto just smiled. He showed no desire to change.

Alice and I sang some songs we had sung about thirty years before, when we were still teenagers. It brought back touching memories. Then she sang a song alone. The words told plaintively about being broken-hearted from loneliness. I sat spellbound, hardly moving a muscle. I visioned Alice spending twenty-five years in Siberia. Otto just smiled. I thought he must have a heart of stone. Nothing seemed to move him anymore.

Once again I asked if we could pray before leaving. He smiled and said, "Yes".

We all prayed fervently that Otto would put his life into the hands of God; otherwise we would never see him again. Also we asked God to be with us on our way home. Marie's and Rudi's difficulty in breathing frightened me, and we leaned hard on God for strength for them.

By this time our taxi was waiting to take us to the train depot, and we had to say good-by.

While riding the train toward home, we began to talk about our papa.

"I am sure," Rudi said, "that he is with the Lord by now. The war is over for more than thirty years. I remember how he talked to me as a young man, telling me I should accept Jesus as my Saviour. I didn't understand what it was all about at that time. Now, by the grace of God, I can say the Lord is my Saviour, and I am ready for heaven also. Lilli, there is a great day coming when all who love Jesus will meet before the throne of God. The Bible says, 'After this I beheld, and, lo, a great multitude, which no man could number, of all nations, and kindreds, and people, and tongues, stood before the throne, and before the Lamb, clothed with white robes, and palms in their hands' " (Revelation 7:9).

I could not hold back the tears of gratitude to hear Rudi and Marie, *born again and returned*, talking about meeting Papa in heaven.

XVI

THE HIDDEN BIBLE

During my month's stay with Marie and Rudi in West Germany, two families dropped in unexpectedly. They had been friends of Marie and Rudi in Russia.

These two families, the Albrechts and the Hinkes, stayed with us for three days. Thanks to the unoccupied, five-bunk bedroom the landlord allowed us to use, we were able to have our guests with us nights as well.

Those were three wonderful days of Christian fellowship. Each evening we gathered for services in the large room, as neighbors also joined us for singing, preaching, and prayer.

Blessings flowed during those meetings. So did tears—tears of gratitude to God for bringing these dear ones through all their sufferings.

The Albrechts had two daughters, Karen and Irene, ten and twelve years old. I talked to the girls about Jesus. That evening, after the meeting closed, these two and Inge from next door asked if they could talk with me. I took them into a room alone, and they began to cry. They wanted to know how they could be saved from their sins. After I explained the way of salvation, all three girls gave their hearts to the Lord. Soon the Albrecht parents came into the room and rejoiced with us. Then together all of us knelt to thank God for saving these three souls.

Inge's parents had been to the meeting also, but had gone home. Karen, Irene, Inge and I went over to share her decision with them. Inge rushed into her mother's arms and asked for her forgiveness. We all prayed again, and again there were tears of joy.

When we arose from our prayer, I noticed Rita, Inge's sixteen-year-old sister, standing in a corner of the room looking very sad. I went to her and asked if she loved Jesus. She began to weep, saying "I would like to give my heart to Jesus too."

Once more we all went to our knees, and Rita gave her heart to Jesus. All eight of us prayed, and then I taught the girls the chorus "Zu sein wie Jesus" (To Be Like Jesus). The hour being very late, we reluctantly said good-night.

In the morning there was much to talk about. Irene said, "I feel so good on my first morning as a Christian. All my fear is gone. I know Jesus forgave me all my sins, and now when He comes again I know I won't be left behind. I never knew it was so easy to become a Christian."

Karen said, "Now I understand why Jesus died on the cross for sinners like me. I am so happy that I know Jesus."

Parents and daughters rejoiced together. I looked on happily, thankful to have a part in the precious experience.

The three days with our guests went all too fast, and we had to say good-by. Saying good-by always has its sad side. On the other hand, saying good-by to Christian friends can make heaven more meaningful, for in heaven there will be no partings.

Although Marie and Rudi had made many fine Christian friends in their little town in Germany, they longed for their old friends whom they had known in Russia. With these they could share the heartaches of the past and the struggles of adjusting to life in Germany.

Sensing Marie and Rudi's loneliness, I asked them if we might visit some of their friends who had also returned and were now in Germany. The idea pleased them greatly, and we began talking over possible plans. If we would go to Bertha's home, a two-hour train ride away, we could visit not only with her but also with a number of others living near her.

Bertha and her family gave us a warm Christian welcome. Knowing of our coming, they had arranged for a home service that Saturday evening. Two ministers had already arrived ahead of us. In a short time a large room was filled with people who had recently returned from Russia.

Customarily, three or four ministers preach at such a meeting. Between preaching they sing a song, and when all the preaching is over, they kneel for prayer.

On this particular evening, three ministers preached. All three sermons brought blessings to us. They plainly brought blessing to others also, for when the last speaker gave an altar call, three boys gave evidence that they wanted to know Jesus as their personal Saviour.

We all knelt, and everyone in that large room prayed. The three boys who had raised their hands sincerely asked Jesus to forgive their sins. Overwhelming joy filled the room.

"Oh, I wish I could stay in Germany among these people," I told myself. "They are so open to the Gospel—especially the young people." One of them, Little Rosemarie, said she had accepted the Lord just one week before this, and she added, "Now I feel joy in my heart like never before. I feel like telling everybody about it. I am so thankful to live in Germany. Now I can talk about my Jesus freely.

A man named Kurt, who was present that night, had been a truck driver in Russia. He related this pathetic experience:

"One cold, rainy day as I was driving my truck, I saw a little girl, perhaps ten years old, running in the woods. I stopped and asked her where she was going. She was so frightened and was crying so hard that she couldn't answer me. I was going to drive off, but somehow I couldn't. I stopped again, took the little girl in my arms, and set her beside me in the truck. I told her I loved Jesus. Then she started to tell me what was on her heart.

" 'My mother is in the hospital very sick,' she said. 'I have been living with my aunt. When I told her I love Jesus she said I had to leave. She's afraid to keep a Christian in her home. It's twenty miles to the hospital where my mother is, and I want to get there before she dies. I want to talk to my mother, at least a couple of words.' "

" 'Twenty miles!' I exclaimed. 'Little girl, that is a long way.'

"She was already wet from the rain and shivering from the cold. She had no coat. I felt so sorry for her that I took her to the hospital. But we were too late. Her mother had passed away. I will never forget the little girl's brokenheartedness. She wrung her little hands and cried, 'Oh, Mother, oh Mother! Why did you leave me here? I wanted to talk to you, at least a couple of words.' Then, turning to me, she asked, 'Where can I go now? Will someone take care of me? I lost my papa. We never heard from him after the war. He must be dead too.' "

By this time nearly everyone in our prayer meeting was in tears.

"I would have loved to have kept her," Kurt said, "but nobody can adopt a child in Russia. Not daring to show the compassion I felt, I had to deliver that little Christian girl to an unchristian orphange. Ever since then I carry a heavy burden for her. I wonder, could we all just now join our hands and pray that God will strengthen her in that orphanage, and that she will be able to keep her faith in Jesus until she is grown up?"

Gladly we all agreed to pray for her.

After the meeting I visited with Konrad, one of the ministers.

He told me, "When I was released from Russia and returned to West Germany, I was very much surprised at the good conditions in which people were living. But as I looked for a church that would meet my need, I found churches very cold spiritually. I could not understand why these churches here in Germany were so cold. Why did the Christians not pray more? Everyone seemed to be in such a hurry. They were even driving automobiles. In Russia we gladly walked many hours to be in church services, and the services always lasted a couple of hours. Why did the services in Germany last only one hour? And why did people whisper to each other before services started?

"All of this I was not used to, and it was very hard on me. I was hoping the believers in a land of freedom would be on fire for God. But, sad to say, this I could not find here, and my soul began crying out with the Psalmist, 'As the hart panteth after the water brooks, so panteth my soul after thee, O God' (Psalm

42:1).

"I began to long to go back to Russia. There the believers in some places were in fear because of persecution, but they were on fire for God."

After a pause he asked, "Lilli, how are the churches in America?"

"I can happily say that the church in America seems more spiritual than in Germany," I told him. "People are becoming more hungry for the Word of God and for a closer fellowship with true believers. Still, I can feel with you, Brother Konrad. I have experienced that myself. We had to search to find a church that was alive spiritually, where the Holy Spirit was moving."

Brother Konrad went on, "Although I felt a longing to go back to Russia because I missed the church, God supplied in a different way. In the several years since I came, thousands of German believers have returned to West Germany. Now we have our own services all over West Germany, and we rejoice in the rich spiritual fellowship."

Hymns meant much to these Christians. I noticed nearly all the people at that prayer meeting had handwritten songbooks, put together with songs mailed to them by friends. They read each one over and over. And when they sang, they would never think of omitting a stanza. Even if it had many stanzas, they sang them all, so great was their hunger for the Word of God.

One lady, named Lydia, showed me her songbook after dismissal. I noticed it was spotted with tears. She said as she turned its pages lovingly, "This is the third book I have copied by hand. Twice my book was destroyed by unbelievers."

I asked her, "Was your Bible destroyed also?"

"No," she said. "But I know of another town where they searched for Bibles. One lady had one. As she prayed and wondered how to hide it before the officer arrived, the thought came to her to bake a cake and put the Bible in it. Quickly she mixed the cake. Carefully she laid her Bible in it and baked the strange mixture. When the officers came, they searched everywhere but found no Bible."

Another lady, Alma, who had lived twenty-six years in Russia, said, "We had only one Bible in the whole village where I lived. No officer asked us if we had a Bible. We shared that Bible so every family could read it for one or two days at a time. In other towns or villages, people took out pages from their Bibles and shared them with people who didn't have any. In our village the government offered us a building where we were allowed to worship on Sundays and during the week. The building was very small so if I wanted to be inside for service, I had to be there two hours before it started. People would stand outside and listen through the window. We were so thankful we did not need to be afraid. Our authorities were very good to us. We did not have any trained ministers. After a man accepted Jesus as his Saviour, if he lived close to God and was a good example as a Christian, he could preach."

A number of the Christians added, "If a village or a city had good-hearted authorities, the believers did not suffer. Although religion was supposedly free in Russia, the degree of freedom was dependent upon the authorities in charge."

Bertha had lived in an area of Russia which had not had friendly authorities.

"Our neighbors planned a wedding," she recalled. "They invited a thousand people."

"A thousand people!" I exclaimed. To me this seemed almost unbelievable.

"Yes, they invited a thousand people. They invested all they had in preparing food for that many people. Choirs and a brass band were invited. Two men were engaged to preach. The parents hoped that by gathering all these people together for a wedding ceremony, they would hear the Gospel and some would accept Jesus as their Saviour. But when the ceremony began, the police appeared. Although the bride and groom went to them and begged for mercy, telling them everything was prepared, the police did not listen to their pleading. Neither the guests nor the family were able to enjoy it."

I really enjoyed my visit with these German

Christians, but too soon we had to say good-night. The next morning, Sunday, the group met again for another prayer meeting and sermons by Rudi and two other ministers. I was so blessed to hear these people pray, knowing how much they had gone through. I was reminded of Psalm 125:1: "They that trust in the Lord shall be as mount Zion, which cannot be removed, but abideth for ever."

"Lilli," Bertha asked after dismissal, "would you like to have the children together sometime for a children's meeting?"

I gave Bertha an emphatic, "Yes, I would like very much to do that."

Bertha thought a little. "Sunday afternoon is a good time for children to get together. Let's plan for it this afternoon."

Eleven children came, ranging in age from nine to thirteen. All had been born in Russia.

At the beginning of the session, I asked them how they liked Germany.

"We love it," they all said. "It's just great. Now we have Sunday school, and we can go to church and study the Bible and pray as much as we like."

I taught them an English chorus, "The Lord Is My Shepherd," and told them the story of Moses. We sang more songs and then prayed. To my surprise, all eleven prayed. Irmgart, the youngest, prayed for the first time in her life. It thrilled me to see what God was doing among these children, and I thanked Him for letting me work with them that afternoon.

In the evening an informal group including two missionaries from America, met at Bertha's where we sang with accompaniment for three hours. The meeting brought nostalgic memories of my childhood days at home.

On Monday our three-day stay at Bertha's came to an end. It had been a wonderful time of fellowship, not only with the family, but also with their many Christian friends with whom we had visited and prayed. After we prayed together, Bertha's husband took us to the train depot.

Arriving at the apartment, we learned that across the hall from us an elderly Mr. Reschke was very sick. That evening Marie and I went to see him and his wife. In talking with him, I soon realized he had a deep longing in his soul. He asked us to sing, and we did. Then we prayed. As we left I asked him if he would like us to come again.

"Oh, yes, please come," he almost begged.

The next evening all three of us went to see Mr. Reschke. He asked us to sing again, and named some special songs that he liked. After singing, we prayed. Then, to our great surprise, Mr. Reschke prayed, asking Jesus to come into his heart. His wife had known Jesus for many years. Now she witnessed the miracle of her seventy-year-old husband's salvation.

After we left he prayed again. We could hear him from the hallway. I said, "Praise

God! Another soul has come into the kingdom. The angels in heaven are rejoicing."
A second miracle took place that evening also. The Lord healed Mr. Reschke's body. The next day he was walking around and feeling fine.

In the four weeks with Marie and Rudi, I learned that they really loved Jesus. I also learned that Rudi was a good preacher. He preached wherever we went for a visit, and when friends dropped in to see us, he preached also. We had many blessed hours together as we shared Jesus.

My four weeks went by fast, almost too fast, and the time came when only one more day was left. Friends came to say good-by to me. Marie had to go to the doctor, and Rudi had to go with her, so my last full day with them was broken up. Then, for some reason, the doctor could not take care of everything in one appointment, and he booked them again for the next morning, the very time I had to leave for America. This was hard on Marie. She said, "When you came, we failed to meet you at the train depot, and now we really did want to be there to see you off."

I reminded Marie that maybe this was the way God planned to protect her from getting too excited. Excitement was bad for her heart, which had become weak from her many years of working in the mines.

The next morning before separating we joined hands in prayer. We felt the Lord very near.

Marie and Rudi had to leave first. I watched them walk down the street until they turned the corner. Minutes later my taxi came and took me to the train depot. I rode the train to Frankfurt and boarded the plane.

On my way home, my thoughts turned back to the kindred warmth of the past month—a warmth that had bridged thirty years as though they had never been. I felt I knew Marie and Rudi intimately again. They had shared with me the heartaches and sorrow of their long stay in Russia, and I had seen how loneliness, age, and failing health were leaving their marks. On the other hand they had shared their joy in Christ, and I had seen how happiness in Christ was keeping their spirits strong and helping them face life with courage and serenity.

I tried to express their feelings in this poem that I dedicate to them.

> We praise our heavenly Father
>   For guiding us by His hand.
> We worship and adore Him
>   On our way to the promised land.
> We long for home and heaven
>   And wish it would be tomorrow
> When we could say good-by to all
>   Our heartache and our sorrow.
>
> We long to be with Jesus
>   And see His blessed face.

    Forever we will praise Him
        For saving us by His grace.

Many times during my visit in Germany,
Christians who had returned from Russia told
me how eagerly they had looked to us in
America for prayer help in their behalf. And
ever since then I have had a great burden for
the suffering Christians around the world.

XVII

ALICE

Two months after returning to America a letter came from Alice. "Otto is in the hospital," she wrote. "His life cannot last much longer unless God performs a miracle. I've told him I want to help take care of him at the hospital, and he is barely allowing me to. His only desire seems to be to see our daughter Selma before he dies. Selma, you know, is still in Russia. He has not seen her since she was a baby, and now she is married and has a family."

"What a tragedy!" I thought. "Suffering brought on by war is terrible. But suffering brought on by unfaithfulness in a husband must be even worse. Poor Alice! She knows both kinds."

I could see Alice standing brokenhearted by Otto's bedside, silently praying, waiting to hear one kind word from him, one word of love and appreciation for her, one sign of acceptance of her as his wife; and more yet, one word of prayer to the Father in heaven.

"We received word from Selma," I read further in Alice's letter, "that she and her family were ready to leave Russia for West Germany. We were tremendously excited. It's twenty-seven years since Otto has seen her.

"Then one afternoon, after rushing home from the hospital to see whether they had come, I found Selma and her family! No greater joy could have come to me than to greet them at a time like that, when I most needed help and comfort. There is no greater love than God's love, and God had answered my prayer that they would return and could be with me.

"Selma felt deep distress over the news of her father's illness, and soon we all rushed to the hospital.

"The meeting was touching. Otto was still able to recognize his daughter, and was very happy to see them all. He was even able to visit with them a little during the next several hours. Then they had to leave the hospital for the night.

"The next morning on their return, they found he could not speak any more. Selma cried, 'Father, Father! Please speak to me one more word.' But it was too late.

"One hour later Otto slipped into eternity, and as far as anyone knows he was not ready for heaven.

"God had been good to him by extending his life until Selma's return, and by having many people witness to him, but he never openly repented. It was very hard to see him die without Jesus, but how thankful I was to have my daughter with me, so I did not have to go through the grief all alone. And now my daughter and family own that beautiful home Otto had built."

Reading Alice's letter brought me sadness as I recalled her hard life in Siberia where she was even thankful for frozen potatoes. Also the letter brought me happiness. I rejoiced to hear that Selma and family had arrived when Alice needed help and comfort most. To me this was a miracle. I broke into tears thinking how much our heavenly Father loves us and how He makes our burdens lighter.

XVIII

FIVE CARNATIONS

Soon after my visit with Marie and Rudi, I realized from their letters that their health was getting poorer. I began to wonder, "Will I ever be able to see them again?"

Two years went by. Then an announcement came in the mail from West Germany.

"A rally is planned in Wiesbaden, West Germany on June 5-6, 1976." It was signed by a member of the *Brüche zur Heimat* (Bridge to the Homeland) Mission. A postscript to me personally read, "We would love to see you too, Lilli. You will find us in the rally building selling our Bibles, songbooks, and other religious books those two days."

"Mother!" I said eagerly, "A rally is planned! A rally for all Germans who have returned from Russia and other countries! A refugee committee supported by the West German government invites all of these to come together in a big building in Wiesbaden. Here many people will have a chance to meet again."

Mother grew excited with me.

"How wonderful it would be for me to go,

Mother! I might meet many dear friends that were scattered through the war. For Marie and Rudi's sake, I should go anyway. This is a second good reason for going. The invitation comes from the *Brücke zur Heimat,* that Mission that helped us by sending us forms for our visas to America. Remember?"

We thought, prayed, and planned, and almost before I knew it, I found myself on the Luft Hansa soaring toward Germany.

Again Marie and Rudi did not meet me at the train depot. My plans had been made so fast that I could not let them know the exact time of my arrival.

"We didn't meet you the last time," Marie apologized, along with her warm greeting. "This time we didn't again."

All three of us understood why, and we soon turned our conversation to happy things ahead.

"We plan to go to the rally too," Marie announced with pleasure.

"Good!" I said. "We can go together, can't we?"

"We already have bus tickets for the three of us," they told me. "Yes, indeed, we'll go together."

Arriving at the large building in Wiesbaden, I stood in amazement for several moments. Thousands of people were moving among each other, looking hopefully for friends or relatives whom they had not seen for many years. I thought, "Oh, will I not recognize at least one friend?"

As we joined the crowd I suddenly came face to face with Martha, the daughter of Susanna and Albert whom I had visited five years before this. At that time Martha and Albert had been in Germany just one month and I remembered they had been very bewildered in their new culture.

Now greeting them warmly, I asked, "And how do you like Germany?"

Martha smiled broadly. "Oh, much better than at first."

Their happy smiles helped me feel free to ask another question, "Did you buy a home?"

"Yes," she replied, "and we have it almost paid for."

"How wonderful!" I said. "And how nice you look, both of you! Well-dressed and happy!"

"Thank you, Lilli. We have adjusted to our new life in Germany."

Albert added, "To me the people here looked so wealthy, and we felt so poor, when we first came from Russia. We felt we did not fit. But now it is home to us."

We separated then and moved on to try to find other old friends.

Seeing a church organization selling books, I asked about a mission named *Brücke zur Heimat*.

"Oh, no," they told me. "We are a Lutheran Church organization."

I walked a while and found another relgious

book-selling center. Here I made the same inquiry.

"Oh, no," I was told again. "We are a Catholic organization. We don't know anything about a *Brücke zur Heimat* mission."

Finally I took courage to ask at the information center for paging service.

Still receiving no answer, I began asking people at random about the mission. Finally a man told me, "Oh, yes, I know that mission. It's outside this building under a large tree. A group of Christians are singing, and I heard a man preaching also."

All excited, I hurried outside and began winding my way in and out among the crowds there. After a while I heard Gospel singing. In the distance I saw the singers under a tree. I almost ignored etiquette in my hurry to push through the masses toward those singers.

"Brother Wessel," I greeted, rushing toward him, "I found you at last."

"Sister Lilli," he greeted in return. "You came all the way from America. It is so good to see you."

"And it is ever so good to see you. I almost didn't find you. I've been looking for you for hours. You said on the invitation that I would find you in the building. Why are you out here?"

Brother Wessel's face clouded a little as he explained. "We were not allowed to set up our center in the building. We learned after we came that the building was reserved for selling literature of certain denominational groups. Since we are non-denominational, they felt it might cause confusion if we were allowed to sell there also."

After visiting pleasantly with this group for a while, I went on. I wondered how many more friends I might find among the thousands of people that made up these crowds.

I found enjoyment in watching others meet old friends also. Touching scenes were everywhere. I saw people who had not seen each other for thirty-five or forty years fall into each other's arms, tears of joy rolling down their faces.

As I stood there and watched the moving masses, my heart ached within me. Some looked happy, others very sad. I thought "These people need Jesus. Do they know He loves them? Do they know He cares? Was there anyone to tell them?"

Then I thought of that reminder Jesus gave to His disciples, "The harvest truly is plenteous, but the labourers are few; Pray ye therefore the Lord of the harvest, that he will send forth labourers into his harvest" (Matthew 9:37, 38).

Overwhelming joy came to me when a group of friends gathered around me whom I had not seen for twenty-eight years. One dear friend among them had become a Christian and was now happy in Jesus. He said to me, "We are having a baptismal service at Massen next Sunday, and I invite you to that very special service. It is going to be just like our baptismals in Russia."

I said wistfully, "I'd love to come."

We had much to talk about as we went home from the rally. Never had any of us experienced anything like it. Now we knew better who of our old friends were enjoying freedom in their homeland. We knew which ones had become Christians. We knew better how to pray for each other.

Later in the week we began thinking about the baptismal service on the coming Sunday. I asked Marie, "How far is it?"

I was told, "Massen is about three hours from here by car."

We longed to go, but with Marie's poor physical condition, how could we?

Then on Saturday evening a man named Wilfred came to us and offered, "My wife and I are going by car to Massen tomorrow. We have room for two. If you would like to come along, you are welcome.

"But then one of us would have to stay home," I said.

"Lilli," Rudi offered, "I will gladly stay home. It would make me happy if you and Marie could go."

Marie felt able for the trip, and believing that God had sent Wilfred to us, we accepted.

"We should start a little before 5:00 in the morning," Wilfred figured. "The service begins at 8:00 and we need around three hours for the drive."

Arriving at Massen, we learned that the baptism would be held three miles farther on, where a swimming pool had been rented for a baptistry.

Here were gathered hundreds of believers from all parts of West Germany who had come out of Russia. As we came together around the swimming pool, they took their little songbooks from their pockets and began to sing, though it was a half-hour before the service was to begin. Then came the twenty-two candidates for baptism, all dressed in white, along with four ministers. The candidates were all young men and women.

"They all look so humble," I thought. They have given their lives to Jesus. Now they are willing to follow Him the rest of their lives. Revelation 7:13 and 14 seemed to be happening right before me: "What are these which are arrayed in white robes? and whence came they? And he said to me, These are they which came out of great tribulation, and have washed their robes, and made them white in the blood of the Lamb."

The four ministers took turns preaching. Between sermons the congregation and the choir sang hymns.

Each minister spoke touchingly, in keeping with the occasion. Each one mentioned that in Russia they had had to baptize secretly; in the wintertime braving icy, snowy rivers.

"Now we are free!" they exclaimed, still hardly able to comprehend their freedom themselves. Again and again they shouted out, *"Wie gross ist doch die Liebe Gottes!"* (How great is the love of God!)

As I stood there by that swimming pool, watching those precious new saints being baptized, verses from Psalm 126 became very real to me. "When the Lord turned again the captivity of Zion, we were like them that dream. Then was our mouth filled with laughter, and our tongue with singing: then said they among the heathen, The Lord hath done great things for them. The Lord hath done great things for us; whereof we are glad. They that sow in tears shall reap in joy. He that goeth forth and weepeth, bearing precious seed, shall doubtless come again with rejoicing, bringing his sheaves with him."

Most of the candidates had been converted in Russia, with the help of the four ministers who were now officiating. "How marvelous!" I thought. "And now they can be baptized in freedom."

The entire service by the pool, including singing, preaching, and baptism, lasted two hours. Young and old, many of them stooped from hard labor in Siberia, gladly stood through it all, rejoicing in their liberty to worship the Lord.

I asked Marie, "Wasn't this long service too hard on you?"

"Oh, my dear sister," she said, "we are used to that. In Russia we had a little church building that held only three hundred people. We were nine hundred members. Most of the time we took all the seats out and stood shoulder to shoulder for many hours to listen to the Gospel."

I thought, "Oh, my God! Am I really thankful enough? In America we have the most beautiful churches, but many of them are empty."

From the pool the assembly worked its way into a rented church building for the completion of the service. Here all four ministers preached again, more hymns were sung, and periods for open prayer were fitted in between the preaching.

What moving, heartbroken prayers those people prayed! Most of them had family members still in Russia. Their great prayer-burden was that God would keep the doors open until all would be released.

After the last minister spoke, the newly-baptized group was asked to come to the front. There they knelt around the altar while the ministers laid hands on them, prayed for them, and received them into church fellowship. Then followed their first communion.

After communion, each candidate was presented with a bouquet of five lovely pink carnations, along with three religious pictures containing appropriate Bible verses. At this time also they were greeted with a warm handshake and the kiss of peace—girls with girls, and boys with boys.

Sometime after dismissal I noticed that the

two ministers who did the baptizing had received five carnations also. Since I had never seen a minister presented with flowers, I asked one of them, "Why did you receive the flowers?"

His answer was, "This is just a custom we have observed for many years."

I felt highly honored to be able to shake hands with these ministers who had been imprisoned and had suffered for the cause of Christ. Their comments to me renewed my awareness that while religion was supposedly free in Russia, the degree of freedom depended on the authorities in charge.

Although the complete service had taken five hours, there were no complaints. Here were people more hungry for the Gospel than for food.

From the church we went to the home of a very dear friend of Marie's. Many other friends gathered there also. To my pleasant surprise, one of the first things they did was to take out their songbooks and enjoy a time of singing together. Though their music was not professional, I could feel that every word was as powerful to them as a sermon. I noticed how they cherished their little songbooks, even though they were very simple, without notes of any kind.

The effects of that Sunday lingered with me, especially the preaching. Such preaching I have never heard elsewhere. The sermons somehow radiate a deep appreciation for what

God has done, and are worded in a very simple, humble way. I always saw many tears during every service.

We arrived at home by early evening. It had been a long day, and I was greatly concerned about Marie. She had been troubled with chest pains. Still, she complained very little. The Lord had surely given her needed strength.

We had much to share with Rudi, who was greatly interested in our account of the day's blessed events. Then, supposing we would go to church again that evening, I asked Marie, "How many services do you have in your church on Sundays, and how long do they last?"

"We have only one service," she said. "It's on Sunday morning and it lasts one hour."

Surprised and disappointed, I asked, "Don't you have Sunday school?"

"Yes, we have Sunday school, but only for children."

Now I could see why the Christians who had returned from Russia liked to have their own services. They did not want to be limited to one hour. If the service took five or even six hours, they loved it. They never watched the clock. Praise to the Lord and food for their souls were most important to them.

All too soon my four-week stay with Marie and Rudi ended. Leaving them was difficult on the one hand, considering their poor physical health. Still I was happy for their excellent spiritual health. All three of us knew that if we never met again on this earth, we would surely meet in heaven."

XIX

FAREWELL TO RUDI

Ever since World War II, the West German government showed much interest in helping German people who returned from other countries. In later years it offered special help to those who returned from Russia, giving them money to help them start again.

Marie and Rudi benefitted greatly from their move to Germany. They received a good pension and medical and hospital provision. By 1978 they were looking back on five years of freedom. They were enjoying fellowship with many new friends in West Germany, besides keeping in contact with old ones who had also returned from Russia. And they were looking forward to moving into the new house they were building together with Rudi's niece and family.

Rudi, with his health failing faster than Marie's, had a special longing to move into the new house. God, however, had other plans for him. Just one month before the house was ready for occupancy, Rudi became very ill. Doctors discovered cancer that had spread beyond control.

Marie sent the sad news to us here in America: "Doctors can do no more. Rudi probably will not be with us long unless God performs a miracle."

I was very much concerned for Marie—for twenty years, now, an emphysema sufferer. Would she now be able to take the loss of Rudi?

I asked myself, "Shall I go to them? I would love to see Rudi before he passes on, and I could be a help to Marie. If I go, then at least one from our family will be there to share the grief. I can hardly bear to think of Marie standing all alone at the graveside of her husband whom she loved so dearly."

During the two weeks I prayed much about this, a letter and a telephone call from Marie told us his condition was becoming more and more critical. Then the door opened for me to go.

"Will I still find Rudi alive when I get there?" I wondered.

Marie opened the door, discovered me, ran back to the bedroom, then returned to greet me.

'Lilli!" she cried, grabbing me in a clinging embrace.

"Is Rudi still alive?" I asked.

"Yes, he's been asking for you the last couple of weeks. That was why I ran to the bedroom first. I went to tell Rudi you had arrived."

I followed her to the bedroom to greet

Rudi. My heart ached at the sight of him. He looked like only skin and bones.

"Rudi, how are you?" I asked him.

"Rejoicing in the Lord," he answered, "Oh, it is wonderful to be so near to eternity."

"Are you in a lot of pain?"

"Yes," Rudi replied, "but I feel supported through the prayers of my brothers and sisters in Christ."

Grief and joy mingled into one during my week there before he passed away. Once he smiled radiantly and raised his hands heavenward. Though his eyes were closed, Marie asked, "Rudi, what have you seen? Your face is shining."

He answered, "Oh, Marie. I saw my beautiful Lord standing by my bed. He just left."

Many times we prayed and sang, both day and night. That was what he most desired. Never did he complain. Always he rejoiced about going home to be with Jesus.

One day while visiting with his niece named Nelly and her two sons, I began talking to the boys about their souls. Both showed great interest and conviction, and right there they confessed their sins, asked God's forgiveness and committed their lives to Him.

With great joy we entered Rudi's room to tell him the good news. The boys knelt at Rudi's bedside and prayed again that God would forgive all their sins so they could meet Uncle Rudi in heaven.

What a touching scene! Tears of joy were flowing as all the rest of us were praying. The angels in heaven were rejoicing also, for Jesus said, "Joy shall be in heaven over one sinner that repenteth, more than over ninety and nine just persons, which need no repentance" (Luke 15:7).

Then Rudi laid his hands on the boys and prayed for them. It made me think of Isaac blessing Jacob, and of Jacob blessing Ephraim and Manasseh.

Just before his death Rudi asked us to sing and pray again. He also prayed. His last whisper was, "Jesus, Jesus, wonderful Jesus." Then he said to the rest of us, "The Lord bless you all," and he slipped into eternity.

The funeral services lasted two hours. Just as people came every day to see him during his last sickness, so now they came from everywhere to pay their last respects to him.

Rudi's body rests in a well-kept cemetery on a hill just a ten-minute walk from the new home they built. Marie, though lonely, takes comfort in knowing his sufferings are over, he is in heaven, and someday she can meet him there.

"And until then," she told me, "at least I can go to his grave now and then. He could have been killed in the war, or he could have died in a prison camp in Siberia, or he could have been killed while working in the copper mine. In any of those cases, his grave, if he had had one, would be far away from me now.

But God in His great mercy has let us live together through those hard years in Russia, and through five enjoyable years here in West Germany. And now He lets Rudi's body rest near me. How good God has been to me!"

I nodded. "Marie, I do think so too. I am happy for you that Rudi could be with you this long."

Then our thoughts turned once more to our own papa. Probably we will never know how he had to suffer, how he died, or how he was buried.

Marie and I could not hide our tears. Then I said, "Marie, what would be left for us if we would not know the Bible is true?"

"Yes, it would be a sad life," Marie replied, "but I am so happy for the promise in I Thessalonians 4:17, "Then we which are alive and remain shall be caught up together with them in the clouds, to meet the Lord in the air: and so shall we ever be with the Lord."

"Let's rejoice, Marie," I said, "for I know Papa will be there, and we know Rudi will be there. Soon you and I will be there also, for Jesus is coming soon!"

The time came for my departure to America. Marie went with me to the train depot. We both looked at each other, wondering whether we would see each other again in this life.

When we saw the train coming, we embraced each other tightly. Then I said, "Marie, I know God will not forsake you. Just take the hand of Jesus. He wants to be your Good Shepherd the rest of your life. Good-by, Marie."

My twelve-hour trip home gave me time to think. I had experienced blessings as well as sorrows. I knew I had been carried by the power of God. And now I was looking forward to passing on to my family Rudi's triumphant last moments. I will always remember his kind, loving personality, his powerful preaching, and his dedicated Christian life.

XX

TO THE AMERICAN PEOPLE, IN LOVE AND APPRECIATION

My first profound impression of America, you remember, came in Germany at the Bremer seaport, hearing that beautiful song, "America, America, God shed His grace on thee."

Other impressions followed. When I arrived in America and received my first American money, I asked about the words and the pictures on it. I was especially pleased with the motto, "In God we trust." I considered it a privilege to handle that kind of money.

Also I heard the President of the United States say openly that he was a Christian and that he read the Bible every day. How different, I thought, from Hitler who made me change my name because it came from the Bible.

Later, when taking night classes in our public school, I was surprised to see a large Bible on a shelf. I asked the teacher, "Do you have Bibles in school?"

"Oh, yes," she said. "Every classroom in America has a Bible." How can I possibly explain what that meant to me as an immigrant? I had not known before what real freedom was. Now in America I found that even public schools had the Word of God.

My first Christmas in America I shall never forget. The many nativity scenes added much to the holiday season. I had never seen anything like that in Germany.

I have one criticism, however, for the American people, and I give it in love. I cannot understand how some of us can throw away so much good food, when in many parts of the world, people are starving to death. Could the reason be that America has always had plenty of food, and people don't know what it means to live with little?

One girl once told me, "I just have a bad habit. I throw food away and don't know why I do it." I was too shocked to answer her. I thought, "Can throwing food away really become a habit?"

My heart goes out in compassion to people who are in need. There are millions today who have to suffer need. How can I help them? The Bible tells me, "Bear ye one another's burdens, and so fulfil the law of Christ" (Galatians 6:2). Once I was one of those millions. Only through God's great mercy am I now living in this nation where there is plenty.

I truly love America. I will try my very best to be a good citizen. The Bible teaches us, "Let every soul be subject unto the higher powers. For there is no power but of God: the powers that be are ordained of God" (Romans 13:1). Also we find in Titus 3:1, "Put them in mind to be subject to principalities and powers, to obey magistrates, to be ready to do every good work."

I have always been impressed with the freedom we have here. In America people are free to worship at the church of their choice, free to vote for the candidate of their choice, free to speak, free to move. Few countries offer such liberties.

Let us all be grateful for this freedom.

Sad to say, some things have changed in recent years. As far as I know, in most of our states the Bibles have been taken out of the public schools. Why did this happen? Could the reason be that we Christians who take the Bible as the Guide for our lives have not done all we could to keep it in our schools? Could it be that we have failed to pray for the leaders in government?

The founders of our nation paid a tremendous price to win the freedom we now enjoy. Let us never think our nation will stand firm if we turn away from God. Without Him our blessings will disappear, our nation will suffer, and tragedy will result.

Let us turn to God for help as never before. The Bible says: "If my people, which are called by my name, shall humble themselves, and pray, and seek my face, and turn from their wicked ways; then will I hear from heaven, and will forgive their sin, and will heal their land" (II Chronicles 7:14).

God has permitted me to go through tragedy in my earlier life. I am thankful for the way He has kept me through it all, sparing my life in times of great danger. When I review the miracles the Lord has done for our family, I wonder: Do I really praise the Lord enough? Or as much as I have promised? Have I been discouraged when maybe I should not have been? I am thankful that God was merciful and loving even when I failed. I find comfort in these words: "My little children, these things write I unto you, that ye sin not. And if any man sin, we have an advocate with the Father, Jesus Christ the righteous: and he is the propitiation for our sins: and not for ours only, but also for the sins of the whole world" (I John 2:1, 2). With the Psalmist David, I can say, "Yea, though I walk through the valley of the shadow of death, I will fear no evil: for thou art with me; thy rod and thy staff they comfort me" (Psalm 23:4).

I cannot keep silent. I must let the world know what God has done for me. I am reminded of Jesus' words in Luke 19:40: "I tell you that, if these should hold their peace, the stones would immediately cry out." It is with such compulsion that I have written these pages.

So ends this account of my life's journey. I don't know how I can possibly praise the Lord enough for being my help in every circumstance, and for working all the miracles I have witnessed. I will let the Psalmist David express my praise.

"Bless the Lord, O my soul: and all that is within me, bless his holy name. Bless the Lord, O my soul, and forget not all his benefits" (Psalm 103:1, 2).

Christian Light Publications, Inc., is a nonprofit, conservative Mennonite publishing company providing Christ-centered, Biblical literature including books, Gospel tracts, Sunday school materials, summer Bible school materials, and a full curriculum for Christian day schools and homeschools. Though produced primarily in English, some books, tracts, and school materials are also available in Spanish.

For more information about the ministry of CLP or its publications, or for spiritual help, please contact us at:

Christian Light Publications, Inc.
P. O. Box 1212
Harrisonburg, VA 22803-1212

Telephone—540-434-0768
Fax—540-433-8896
E-mail—info@clp.org
www.clp.org